Oxford School Shakespeare

The Tempest

Edited by

Roma Gill, OBE
M.A. *Cantab.*, B. Litt. *Oxon*

Oxford University Press

Oxford University Press, Great Clarendon Street, Oxford OX2 6DP

Oxford New York
Athens Auckland Bangkok Bogota Bombay
Buenos Aires Calcutta Cape Town Dar es Salaam Delhi
Florence Hong Kong Istanbul Karachi
Kuala Lumpur Madras Madrid Melbourne
Mexico City Nairobi Paris Singapore
Taipei Tokyo Toronto Warsaw

and associated companies in
Berlin Ibadan

Oxford is a trade mark of Oxford University Press

© Oxford University Press 1998

ISBN 0 19 831998 3 (Schools edition)   1 3 5 7 9 10 8 6 4 2
ISBN 0 19 831999 1 (Trade edition)   1 3 5 7 9 10 8 6 4 2

Illustrations by Martin Cottam

Cover photograph by Donald Cooper shows Rudi Davies as Miranda and Max Von
Sydow as Prospero in the Old Vic's 1988 production of *The Tempest*.

For Ashley

Oxford School Shakespeare
edited by Roma Gill

A Midsummer Night's Dream	The Taming of the Shrew
Romeo and Juliet	Othello
As You Like It	Hamlet
Macbeth	King Lear
Julius Caesar	Henry V
The Merchant of Venice	The Winter's Tale
Henry IV Part I	Antony and Cleopatra
Twelfth Night	The Tempest

Typeset by Herb Bowes Graphics, Oxford
Printed in Great Britain at the University Press, Cambridge

Contents

By Providence divine

You can call it what you like—Fate, Fortune, Destiny, the hand of God . . . It's easy enough to accept in works of fiction, where 'God' is the author and he (or she) is in total control and answerable for all the consequences. In real life it's a different matter—a mystery! Yet when events are so endlessly strange, sometimes there's no other explanation.

Providence must have been on Shakespeare's side in 1610, bringing to his notice a letter from William Strachey in the New World of America. The vessel in which Strachey was sailing had been shipwrecked on the Bermudas, but by some near-miracle the crew and all the passengers had escaped with their lives and been able, eventually, to resume their voyage to Virginia. Strachey ascribed their adventures, both 'wreck and redemption', to the 'gracious and merciful providence of God'—a 'permissive providence' that suffered evil in order that good might ultimately prevail.[1]

Strachey's letter was the starting-point, the springboard, for Shakespeare's imagination. The plots of his most recent plays (*Pericles* (1607–8), *Cymbeline* (1608–9), and *The Winter's Tale* (1611)) had all been dependent on some measure of providential or even supernatural agency; but the sources for these plays had been supplied by existing fictions. The characters had seemed real enough—human beings who thought and felt and suffered just as we do—but their stories had been set in far-off worlds which, although certainly European, had been so remote in time as to be almost unrecognizable. And supernatural intervention, in such circumstances, had not seemed wholly improbable. But now Shakespeare could work with real-life material, with a story that begins in a truth: a genuine tempest and an actual shipwreck.

From such a springboard Shakespeare's imagination bounds higher than ever before, inventing an action that brings together politics, revenge, conspiracy, and romantic love; peopling this with characters from his own and earlier drama; and creating, in Ariel

---

[1] See 'Shakespeare's Sources', p. 89.

and Caliban, two beings never before existing and made—in his own words—from 'airy nothing'.[1]

And even this is not all! In *The Tempest*, and in the other three plays of this final period of his dramatic activity, Shakespeare's thoughts are occupied with serious themes—the related topics of loss and restoration, injury and healing, fault and forgiveness. Time, here, is of the very essence—Time, which had been a constant fascination for Shakespeare throughout his entire career, in its many operations as destroyer and ravisher, healer and restorer. In Prospero, omniscient and manipulative, the play's leading and most complex character, some readers (and spectators) have found the playwright himself—or at least some part of him. I cannot believe that the dramatist's whole philosophy of life is represented by the conjuror's explanation that the human characters, like the spirits, are no more than 'such stuff As dreams are made on' (4, 1, 156–7)—but I am tempted, fancifully, to take Prospero's epilogue for Shakespeare's own farewell to his life in the London theatre. The duke pleads with the audience to be released from confinement on the island so that he can continue with his own life beyond the boundaries of the stage and the text: Shakespeare, although he continued to write, seems to have been spending more and more time in his home town of Stratford-upon-Avon. After *The Tempest* there were no more complete plays from his pen.

---

[1] Shakespeare gave his own description of the act of poetic creation in *A Midsummer Night's Dream*:

> The poet's eye, in a fine frenzy rolling,
> Doth glance from heaven to earth, from earth to heaven;
> And, as imagination bodies forth
> The forms of things unknown, the poet's pen
> Turns them to shapes, and gives to airy nothing
> A local habitation and a name   (5, 1, 12–17)

Leading Characters in the Play

Prospero The real Duke of Milan, deported from his kingdom by a jealous younger brother who usurped his throne. A devout student of magic arts, he has perfected his skills during twelve years of exile on a lonely island where he lives with his daughter and the island's previous occupant. He is a complex character, a man who has been very badly hurt but who now has the means to revenge his wrongs. His name means 'fortunate, prosperous, successful'.

Miranda Prospero's daughter, whose name means 'wonderful, to be wondered at'. She was three years old when she was deported with her father and now, aged fifteen, she has no knowledge of other human beings. Educated on the island by her father, she is innocent and docile—but she is also mature, and sexually aware.

Alonso The King of Naples, partner in the political coup that overthrew Prospero and made Milan subject to Naples.

Ferdinand Alonso's son who, believing his father to have been drowned in the shipwreck, assumes that he is now King of Naples.

Antonio Younger brother to Prospero and now, through his own treachery, Duke of Milan.

Sebastian Younger brother to Alonso. By nature he is indolent, but he can easily be influenced and led astray by Antonio.

Gonzalo A nobleman from the court of Naples. Although he had been powerless to resist Alonso and Antonio when they overthrew Prospero, he had been able to provide the castaways with the necessities for living—including Prospero's books.

Ariel Prospero's agent on the island. He—or she—is pure spirit, and was composed by Shakespeare out of many traditions and beliefs, ranging from classical mythology to English folklore, and from medieval theology to the theories of contemporary magicians. Before Prospero came to the island, Ariel—who is without size or shape but capable of assuming every shape and size—had been held in captivity for twelve years by the witch Sycorax.

Caliban The barely-human son of Sycorax, exiled to the island at least twelve years before Prospero's arrival there. He must now, at the beginning of the play, be more than 24 years old.

With the exception of Prospero, the real-life characters can be recognized as variants of the stock dramatic types—the chaste maiden, the ardent lover, the cruel brother, the wise counsellor, the drunken servant. They are common to all Elizabethan and Jacobean dramatists, can be found in the Italian *commedia dell'arte*, and trace their origins even further back to the drama of the Romans and Greeks. Among their forebears in Shakespeare's plays are the eponymous lovers Romeo and Juliet, the discontented spoilsport brother Don John in *Much Ado About Nothing*, the long-winded politician Polonius in *Hamlet*. Literature provided Shakespeare with hints and suggestions for Prospero—in Marlowe's Dr Faustus, for example—and life itself produced such personalities as Dr John Dee, the alchemist and physician at the court of Queen Elizabeth, and the European spirit-masters Agrippa (1486–1535) and Paracelsus (1493–1541). Shakespeare himself created the only true ancestor of Ariel—his own Puck in *A Midsummer Night's Dream*—but Caliban, born of intercourse between a witch and a devil, is unique.

Synopsis

Act 1

Scene 1   The tempest and the shipwreck.

Scene 2   The history of Prospero and Miranda; the storm explained; Ariel and Caliban are introduced; Miranda meets Ferdinand.

Act 2

Scene 1   Survivors of the shipwreck: Alonso grieves but Antonio and Sebastian conspire.

Scene 2   Trinculo and Stephano meet Caliban.

Act 3

Scene 1   Ferdinand and Miranda declare their love.

Scene 2   Caliban prompts Stephano and Trinculo to murder Prospero.

Scene 3   The magical banquet with Ariel as harpy; Prospero watches his victims.

Act 4

Scene 1   The betrothal of Ferdinand and Miranda; the celebratory masque; distress of the comic conspirators. Prospero is now fully in command.

Act 5

Scene 1   Renunciation, revelation and reconciliation.

Epilogue

The Tempest: commentary

Pride of place in the Folio of Shakespeare's *Complete Works* is given to the last play he ever wrote. Other plays have more complex characters, more intricate plots, greater poetry—but *The Tempest* is his masterpiece. It is a perfect work of the imagination, where the whole is infinitely greater than the sum of the parts and which commentary, though hoping to enlighten, can never fully explain.

Act 1

Scene 1

The first scene is realistic, creating out of nothing the full force of a storm at sea and the confusions of a ship in distress. Stage directions call for thunder and lightning, and the clipped economy of the prose generates instant urgency: 'Fall to't yarely'. A master of opening scenes, Shakespeare follows his own instructions. *The Tempest* begins in the middle of a crisis, and a catastrophe is achieved in fewer than 100 lines.

But the final throes of a sinking ship are only a small part of the scene's achievement: with the entry of the royal passengers there is a clash of language, manners, and priorities which serves to establish the personalities of most of the play's characters. Alonso's courtesy is quite out of place in this situation, and Gonzalo's insistence on decorum—'remember whom thou hast aboard'—is meaningless. Proper respect is due only to 'these elements': all men are equal at a time like this, and the Boatswain alone has any authority. Alonso seems to recognize this, retiring with Ferdinand to their cabin, where they are later to be joined 'at prayers' by Gonzalo. The old councillor maintains a cheerful good humour to the end, unlike the younger men of the royal party, whose response is only to cast blame on the striving shipmen. Gonzalo has the last word: 'I would fain die a dry death'.

Scene 2

The realism of the first scene is called into question by the first lines to be spoken in Scene 2:

> If by your *art*, my dearest father, you have
> Put the wild waters in this roar . . .

The speaker, Miranda, has also been a spectator of the scene that
we—the audience—have just witnessed. Being so much closer than
we were, she has been so much more moved, and her tender
sympathies are fully aroused. Even when her father, an awe-
inspiring figure in his magician's cloak, tells her that 'There's no
harm done', she cannot silence her distress. But now is the time for
her (and our) enlightenment—and not just about the storm. This
has been no more than 'virtual reality', conjured up by the
scientific magic of Prospero's art.

Laying aside the robe in which his power seems to be invested,
Prospero becomes much more human, a father who sits down with
his teenage daughter to talk to her about their lives together in the
past and the events, twelve years ago, that brought them to this
remote island. Miranda has only the faintest recollection of a time
when there were other people—women—in her baby life, so her
father must begin at the beginning by revealing his identity as Duke
of Milan. And Miranda herself is really a princess. Her question
now is oddly phrased:

> What foul play had we that we came from thence?
> Or blessed was't we did?

Prospero answers her in full:

>   Both, both, my girl.
> By foul play, as thou say'st, were we heav'd thence,
> But blessedly holp hither.

As he proceeds with an explanation, Prospero reassumes his former
dignity, recalling with pride the distinction of his kingdom of Milan
('Through all the signories it was the first') and his own personal
scholarship ('for the liberal arts Without a parallel'). Pride yields to
anger when he recollects his betrayal by the man to whom he had
delegated responsibility, his younger brother and Miranda's 'false
uncle'.

The long narrative begins to lull Miranda, bewildered by this
sudden turn of events, into a semi-hypnotic, semi-magical slumber,
leaving Prospero to re-enact, in his mind and for the benefit of the
audience, the political coup by which he was overthrown and
expelled from his dukedom. His speech grows more passionate as he

recollects the treachery of his brother: the syntax becomes irregular and elisions are frequent—'t'advance', 'chang'd 'em', 'new-form'd 'em', 'i'th' state'. Interrupting himself occasionally to look for his listener, the drowsy Miranda, Prospero returns to the past, which is now present and active in the tenses of his verbs—'thinks me now incapable', 'hearkens my brother's suit'. Miranda is roused to tears and sympathy, eager to prompt her father to more revelations.

Prospero brings the story up-to-date: the expulsion from Milan, abandonment on the sea, and salvation 'By providence divine', whose agent for the purpose had been 'A noble Neapolitan, Gonzalo'. Now Miranda knows all—and the audience can identify the characters involved in the shipwreck. The moment has come for Prospero, after twelve years, to get his revenge! Whilst Miranda yields to the 'good dulness' of irresistible sleep, Prospero re-invests himself with the magic of his cloak and summons the power of his servant-spirit, Ariel.

Immediately the whole scene is lightened: Prospero's impassioned tones, narrating solemn and near-tragic events, give way to Ariel's lively account of his activities in 'performing' the storm to Prospero's command. The verse seems to flicker along with the speaker, whose supernatural manifestation had 'flam'd amazement' throughout the king's ship. Ariel seems to have enjoyed the performance, and Prospero is pleased—especially when he hears that the passengers in the ship have been driven almost to desperation by their fears and torments! But no real harm has come to them: they are all safe ashore, and dispersed around the island.

Prospero now establishes the time of day at about two o'clock in the afternoon—i.e. the time at which any Elizabethan or Jacobean theatrical performance would be expected to start. And the business on which Prospero has embarked must, like a theatrical performance, be accomplished ''twixt six and now'. Shakespeare, apparently, has decided to observe 'the unity of time'[1] with unusual strictness—and to make sure that the audience realizes what he is doing!

First, however, the audience needs some explanation about the wonder-working Ariel, who is now showing a reluctance to undertake any further commissions from Prospero. Such recalcitrance is usual (according to Elizabethan authorities on witchcraft) for the spirits who have been somehow compelled into the service of a magician: their labours are never voluntary, and

[1]   See 'State of the art', p. xxv.

they are always impatient of confinement. Prospero, by reminding Ariel of the exquisite agony from which the spirit has been released, demonstrates his powers and reinforces the contract—and affords Shakespeare opportunity to introduce yet another character, 'the freckled whelp, hag-born', not even 'honour'd with A human shape': Caliban, son of the witch Sycorax. The juxtaposition of Ariel and Caliban forces us to contrast their characteristics—the one light as air and quick as thought, the other heavy, slow and earth-bound.

Miranda, woken from her charmed sleep, is loth to look upon the gross physicality of Caliban, but his existence is necessary for their survival on the island, and her father has power to control even the basest of the elements. Caliban's history, like that of Ariel, is now disclosed to the audience through Prospero's reminders, punctuated with threats from the magician and curses from Caliban. Prospero's arrival on the island had brought liberation, at a price, to Ariel, but enslavement, as he sees it, to Caliban. Miranda, who has hitherto spoken little for herself, surprises now with the vehemence of her attack on Caliban, whose brutish nature had resisted all the efforts that she, as well as her father, had made to educate him in the language and behaviour of civilized human beings. Caliban, unmoved by her words and unrepentant of his actions, trudges off to obey Prospero's commands, constrained by a magical power even stronger than that of his mother and her god. The demonstration of Prospero's skills is now complete, and all but one of the play's major characters has been introduced.

Up to this point the play has been looking back, but now the forward movement begins when Ferdinand, son of the King of Naples, is brought on to the stage. He is still in a dream-like bewilderment following his experiences in the shipwreck, and he has been drawn to Prospero's presence by the sound of Ariel's invisible music. The lyrical lament for a drowned father, and the heartfelt grief of a loving son (even though the audience knows that neither of these is necessary) bring a new gentleness into the play, preparing for a comedy of love rather than a tragedy of revenge.

Prospero directs Miranda's gaze to the first man (apart from himself and Caliban) that she has seen in her twelve years on the island. Miranda admires what she sees, but she is dismissive—' 'tis a spirit': it is nothing more than another of the apparitions conjured up by her father. Reassuring her to the contrary, Prospero seems to withdraw to watch the working-out of his plans. Love is almost instantaneous: Prospero, satisfied, observes that 'At the first sight They have chang'd eyes'—a sure sign (in Elizabethan romantic convention) of the genuine passion. A proposal of marriage is offered with the promise, 'I'll make you The Queen of Naples', but romantic convention now insists on a trial of truth and constancy for Ferdinand's sincerity. The young man's spirit is roused to resist Prospero's threats, and it is undaunted even when his physical strength is overcome by Prospero's magic.

As the happy magician congratulates himself, and applauds Ariel's successes (which will be rewarded with freedom), the uncomprehending Miranda strives to comfort Ferdinand, her first and only love.

Act 2

Scene 1   It is no surprise for the audience to find the survivors of the shipwreck, as Ariel had promised (1, 2, 220), safe on the island. Alonso is grieving for the loss of his son, and refusing the comfort offered by Gonzalo, whom we can now recognize as 'the noble Neapolitan' whose 'gentleness' had provided Prospero with the means of survival—including his books. His efforts now are seconded by another lord, Adrian, but undermined by the sniping wit of Sebastian and Antonio. Gonzalo looks on the bright side: shipwrecks can happen to anyone; they themselves are safe; the island is not nearly as unfit for human habitation as they had expected; their clothes are as good as new . . . Sebastian and Antonio see things differently: to them the air is foul, the grass is brown, and their clothes are damaged. It seems as though they are being deliberately perverse, since Ariel has already testified to the condition of the garments—although the magic of the island is perhaps such that perceptions vary according to the characters: what is green and fresh to the optimistic Adrian and Gonzalo is brown and stained to the scoffers.

Mention of new clothes reminds Gonzalo of the occasion for which they were provided—the wedding at Tunis of the king's daughter, Claribel. But the recollection of this is painful to the king, reminding him that he has lost a daughter as well as his shipwrecked son, and to the discontents Sebastian and Antonio, who remember their opposition to the foreign marriage. Gonzalo reproves their outspokenness: this is not the time or the place for such speech—although he does not deny the truth of what they say. To distract Alonso, Gonzalo begins a meditation (substantially taken from Montaigne's essay 'Of the Cannibals'—see

'Shakespeare's Sources', p. 91) on government and colonization—but his simple naïvety is easily undercut by the quick responses of his hearers. The comfort and banter, even that which is well intended, is beginning to irritate Alonso, and a certain edginess is beginning to set into the jesting. The situation is saved by Ariel and his music, casting a drowsy spell over Gonzalo, the attendant courtiers, and finally reaching even the troubled Alonso.

Antonio and Sebastian, however, are unaffected. In fact Antonio seems to come alive for the first time, showing his true character as he urges Sebastian to follow his own example and take possession of the throne of Naples just as Antonio had usurped the dukedom of Milan from his brother Prospero. Antonio's arguments are witty and persuasive, and Sebastian seems at first to be dazzled by the rhetoric and slow to comprehend the meaning. He is a man of little initiative, but he is all too ready to become an apt pupil. There is only one question: 'But for your conscience?'. This is quickly disposed of with Antonio's characteristic dismissive wit—but the answer confirms Antonio's status as one of Shakespeare's blackest villains. He is guilty of ingratitude, treachery, and, since he intended Prospero's death, fratricide. Completely devoid of all moral principles, he now seeks to win another to join him in infamy.

Disaster is averted with melodramatic promptness. Prospero's all-seeing art has sent Ariel, like the sound of music, to wake the sleepers. They open their eyes to see Antonio and Sebastian with drawn swords, and only some uncharacteristically quick thinking on the part of Sebastian avoids a nasty confrontation. For the present, the danger is over.

Scene 2   The mood of the play shifts into comedy. Caliban, cursing as usual, drags his logs on to the stage but the sound of thunder, like the voice of Prospero, scares him into a momentary silence. Taking the audience into his confidence, he details the many little tricks—petty but painful—with which Prospero can torment his mind and body. At the approach of another person, whom he assumes to be one of the tormentors, Caliban throws himself to the ground and tries to hide beneath his cloak. But there is nothing to fear from Trinculo, whose parti-coloured costume identifies him to the audience as a professional court jester. Desperate to find shelter from the threatening storm, Trinculo discovers Caliban—a 'strange fish' with 'a very ancient and fish-like smell'—and he too takes refuge with the 'monster' under his 'gaberdine'. A second newcomer, Stephano, Alonso's drunken butler, joins the scene so that comedy can develop out of situation and character. At first it is a crude, farcical comedy, laughing at the Elizabethan delight in creatures from the New World, but more serious issues arise when Caliban kneels and worships the 'brave god' with the 'celestial liquor'.

The native inhabitants of the New World presented many ethical problems to the European colonists, and the moral issues were widely debated. Caliban presents himself to Stephano with the same hospitality that he had shown to Prospero twelve years earlier (see *1, 2, 337–8*):

> I'll show thee the best springs; I'll pluck thee berries;
> I'll fish for thee, and get thee wood enough . . .

Although Trinculo mocks, Stephano seizes the offer of service, only too ready to exploit the 'monster'.

Act 3

Scene 1   Like one of the knights in medieval chivalric fiction, Ferdinand sets himself to *earn* the love of his lady, rejoicing in the menial task because it is done for *her* sake. The more he labours, the more Miranda loves. She has stolen out to gaze upon the first young man she has ever seen—and Prospero, from a distance, looks on with approval.

It is the meeting of innocence and experience. The sophisticated Ferdinand knows the conventions of courtship and he is fluent in its vocabulary. From his experience, he can assure Miranda that she is 'perfect' and 'peerless', the abstract of all feminine graces; although he is in fact a prince, for her he is a willing slave; heaven and earth must bear witness to his devotion . . . But the guileless innocence of Miranda knows nothing of such niceties, and easily takes the initiative with a direct question 'Do you love me?' When the response is satisfactory, the consequence, for Miranda, is obvious: 'I am your wife if you will marry me; If not, I'll die your maid'. Still speaking the language of courtly love, Ferdinand salutes her as his 'mistress', but Miranda will leave nothing in doubt: 'My husband then?'

Sealing their contract with a handshake, the lovers separate from each other. And a rejoicing Prospero returns to his 'business'.

Scene 2   Plans for yet another takeover bid! Twelve years ago Antonio overthrew his brother and usurped the dukedom of Milan; here on the island Sebastian, urged on by Antonio, has decided to murder Alonso and take possession of the kingdom of Naples; and now, in a crude and drunken parody of the others, Stephano plots against Prospero. Non-stop drinking has given Stephano, flattered by the servile grovellings of his 'servant-monster', illusions of grandeur which respond readily to Caliban's suggestions. Caliban is showing new depths to his baseness: his tongue has been liberated by the alcohol, and with vindictive impotence he exhorts Stephano to do what he himself dare not do—'brain him . . . or with a log

> Batter his skull, or paunch him with a stake,
> Or cut his weasand with thy knife.

Once again the situation is saved by the intervention of Ariel—but not before we have seen the worst of mankind. Most of the seven deadly sins have been released in this single, initially comic, scene: anger, pride, gluttony, envy, covetousness, lust—and perhaps sloth too, in Stephano's lazy refusal to hear Trinculo's warnings. Man is barely distinguishable from beast—for even animals can share Caliban's musical appreciation.

Scene 3   From a position high above the stage, invisible to all the other characters but in full view of the audience, Prospero watches with enjoyment the effects of his spells on those who, twelve years ago, conspired his overthrow. After the trauma of the shipwreck, they have been wandering in the pathless wilderness of the enchanted island, searching in vain for the missing Ferdinand. Old Gonzalo, the 'noble Neapolitan', has been made to suffer with the guilty ones, but now his exhaustion brings an end to their searches—but not to their torments.

The magical music introduces something that seems to be a masque of hospitality, which is praised and wondered at even by the cynical Sebastian and Antonio. Alonso is suspicious, but the reassurances of Gonzalo, and his own desperation, encourage him to eat. What follows is an enactment of one of the episodes from the third book of Virgil's *Aeneid*, in which Aeneas and his Trojan companions, having taken shelter on the island of the harpies, were confronted with just such a banquet followed by an equally threatening prophecy. Ariel, appearing as a harpy, explains the signification: harmony, fellowship, and all natural good order—symbolized by the ceremonial banquet—have been disrupted, and those responsible, the 'three men of sin', must be made to appreciate the magnitude of their offences. The injury to Prospero was an affront to the entire scheme of things, and as such it cannot be tolerated by the very elements themselves: unfit to live amongst men, they have even been rejected, vomited up, by the sea. Their only hope now is in repentance and amendment of their ways: 'heart's sorrow, And a clear life ensuing'.

Having commended Ariel for his performance as the harpy, and for his production of this show, Prospero departs from his high vantage-point, leaving his astounded victims to come to terms with this fearsome indictment. Alonso at once acknowledges his guilt— 'O, it is monstrous, monstrous!'; Sebastian and Antonio are defiant; Gonzalo, although it is not clear what he has actually heard, appears to understand what is happening.

Act 4

Scene 1   Prospero is once again the loving father who, as he explains to the rather bewildered Ferdinand, has imposed these tasks on the young lover only to test the strength of his resolution, which will now be rewarded with the 'rich gift' of Miranda. For the past twelve years, all the time they have been on the island, Prospero has been educating Miranda with unusual care (*1*, 2, 172–4) and, it would seem, preparing her for this moment: she is ready to be the bride of a future king of Naples—and Ferdinand, heir to that throne, has shown himself worthy to be her husband. It is a solemn occasion, a formal 'troth-plight' (although Miranda has no words to say for herself), and Ferdinand speaks his vows with proper seriousness.

The solemnities over, however, Prospero celebrates the engagement of the young couple with the kind of masque that was very popular at the English court of King James. In such 'one-off' performances there was music, dance, and, above all, spectacle, which was often rated as highly as the purely verbal content—hence Prospero's injunctions, 'All eyes! Be silent!' Silence is imperative for Prospero's masque, whose actors are to be the spirits, Ariel, and the 'rabble' of 'meaner fellows' under his control: any external noise, and especially speech, would break the magician's spell.

The characters and themes for the court masques were frequently picked out of classical mythology and combined into an entertainment appropriate for a particular occasion. Here the goddess Ceres expresses the thoughts that are uppermost in Prospero's mind, his 'present fancies'. These include not only concern for the health and prosperity of his daughter and Ferdinand, but also his obsession with their premarital chastity. Ceres is most anxious that neither Venus nor her son should be present at this festivity, because they are associated with lust rather than love. Ceres recalls the episode when they conspired with Dis, god of the underworld, to abduct her daughter—as a result of which the whole earth was forced to endure the barrenness and privations of winter. Reassured by Iris that lust has retired from this scene, Ceres joins with the goddess of marriage, Juno queen of the gods, to pour down all the blessings of earthly fertility, and to promise a new year when

> Spring [will] come to you at the farthest,
> In the very end of harvest.

A kind of ballet is in preparation when suddenly it seems as though Prospero has lost his concentration: the masque which his imagination had called into being is disrupted by his recollection of 'the beast Caliban' and the latest conspiracy against his life. Ferdinand and Miranda are both bewildered by this turn of events, but Prospero is quick to assure them that there is no cause for alarm—but now the party is over! His words of comfort, however, soon become a meditation more fitting for an old man at the end of his life than for a young couple embarking on matrimony. Perhaps Miranda and Ferdinand pay no heed to his words once they know that the 'revels now are ended', making the allowance for him that he—rather uncharacteristically—begs from them:

> Bear with my weakness, my old brain is troubled.
> Be not disturb'd with my infirmity.

But although Prospero's meditation on the evanescence of art and the transitoriness of life is beautiful and very moving, it is itself a necessary part of the masque convention, drawing attention to the splendid constructions of the stage designer whilst at the same time dismissing them as ephemeral (see 'State of the art', p. xxv).

Dismissed to their own devices, Ferdinand and Miranda leave Prospero—but he is not alone for long. The benign father who produced magical shows for his children's delight, and the old man who mused on the realities of existence, are both lost in the embittered revenger who is determined to chastise the clumsy 'varlets', Stephano and Trinculo, who have involved themselves with Caliban in this latest attempt on his life. Their conspiracy seems to have taken Prospero by surprise: apart from this, he has been in complete control of all that has happened on the island, stage-managing the other characters as though the play were his own. But the real object of his wrath is, of course, Caliban—who has repaid all Prospero's teaching and training with ingratitude; who has attempted to rape Miranda; and who is now leading others to murder his benefactor.

Prospero's anger is also the disappointed frustration of the Renaissance humanist and educational theorist, once optimistic about the ability of 'nurture' to improve upon, and even transform, 'nature'. Given the same upbringing, such theorists would argue, Miranda and Caliban should have developed into equally praiseworthy personalities. But the theory seems to have failed—not, as Prospero sees it, because of any fault in his own methodology, but because his pupils have been essentially good or bad by nature. Miranda has thrived and will be rewarded, but Caliban, 'a born devil, on whose nature Nurture can never stick', has grown worse with age and must be punished.

When they appear, the malefactors have already suffered considerable discomfort and distress through the misleadings of Ariel. Stephano and Trinculo seem to be wavering in their resolution, but Caliban urges them on, even gaining an ascendancy over them which is expressed first in his speech—verse and not prose—and then in his contempt for their greedy seizure of the 'trumpery' which Prospero has laid as bait for them. Prospero now shows at his vindictive worst, setting 'virtual reality' hounds to drive them from the stage and threatening to torment them all with the same agonies that he had previously used to discipline Caliban.

Now Prospero is a truly terrifying figure: we know that he is able and willing to inflict great pain, and he has given ample demonstration of his power to paralyse and disarm anyone who opposes him. Here, at the climax of the play, he gloats over what he has achieved:

> At this hour
> Lies at my mercy all mine enemies.

Accompanied by Ariel, he quits the stage, leaving the audience—perhaps quite literally—in the dark.

Act 5

Scene 1　It is unusual—and would, indeed, be bad stagecraft—for characters to leave the stage after the end of one scene only to return immediately for the beginning of the next. In this instance, however, it seems probable that the play was intended for an indoor playhouse, and that a substantial break between these two scenes was designed to allow for changing and replacing the candles and torches lighting the hall.

Prospero, wrapped in his magician's cloak, will remain 'invisible' to all except the audience (and, of course, Ariel) until he is ready to disclose himself to the prisoners held captive in his spell. The moment he has been waiting for throughout twelve long years has almost arrived. He makes one last check: everything is in place, and the time is right, 'On the sixth hour'—just four hours after it was first checked with Ariel (*1*, 2, 240), and well within the scope of the 'unity of action'!

We can have no idea, up to this very moment, exactly what it is that Prospero intends to do with his victims. They have been so tortured and tormented that they are almost out of their minds with grief and fear, and now they are held, the innocent as well as the guilty, in a state of total paralysis. Even Ariel, the disembodied spirit incapable of human sympathies, is moved to plead for them, and Prospero seems to be deeply affected by this—perhaps, even, made ashamed of himself and the extremes to which he has pursued his revenge. But now, taught by Montaigne, he has learned the lesson that the greatest of all virtues is achieved by the man who, although 'being touched and stung to the quick with [some] wrong or offence', resists and overcomes the 'furiously-blind desire of revenge' (see 'Shakespeare's Sources', p. 92):

> Though with their high wrongs I am struck to th' quick,
> Yet with my nobler reason 'gainst my fury
> Do I take part. The rarer action is
> In virtue than in vengeance.

He prepares to release the prisoners, imposing just one condition (which in fact is not complied with): 'They being penitent.'

First, however, Prospero must prepare himself to surrender his magic art, with all the skills and delights it has given him, and all the spirits whom he has been empowered to command. For this purpose Shakespeare has given him, cleansed of all sinister implications, the words spoken by Medea in Ovid's *Metamorphoses* (see 'Shakespeare's Sources', p. 92). Medea herself was a witch but Prospero, although he makes large claims for what he has accomplished, dealt only in 'white magic', employing the elemental spirits of nature and not the supernatural, even diabolic, agents of the 'black magic' witches: he has been able to raise the winds and rend the skies, but his 'rough magic' has not had the force to affect the hearts and minds of those who came under its influence. Prospero was able to bring Miranda and Ferdinand together—but it was of their own volition that they fell in love. And although he had raised the tempest that brought his enemies within his power where they could be tormented and confused, lectured and threatened, he has not succeeded in compelling penitence from them. Only Alonso has responded, acknowledging his guilt and accepting as punishment what he believes to be the loss of his son. Sebastian and Antonio have so far been unmoved.

Having said his farewells, Prospero turns his attention to his royal prisoners, who have now been shepherded, still hypnotically entranced, into his magic circle. Fully in control of himself, he can utter his reproaches without the angry excitement that he showed when he first told Miranda of the injuries he had suffered, and he is even able to extend his forgiveness to his brother. When he has been dressed in the clothes that will confirm his identity as Duke of Milan, Prospero confronts his former enemies as they gradually come to their senses. Their waking reactions are all different: Gonzalo is overjoyed, but can hardly believe his eyes; Alonso, offered physical proof of reality, begs forgiveness and promises to make amends for the wrong he has done; but Antonio and Sebastian have few words to say. Perhaps they hear a threat of future blackmail when Prospero assures them that he will 'tell no tales'—for the time being!

The play moves smoothly to its expected closure. Prospero will have his dukedom back, and, in the marriage of Miranda and Ferdinand, Milan will be re-united with the kingdom of Naples. Gonzalo sees in all this the hand of a deterministic providence:

> Was Milan thrust from Milan that his issue
> Should become kings of Naples?

Alonso too, when he hears the Boatswain's report on the safety of their vessel, gives it as his opinion that 'there is in this business more than nature Was ever conduct of'—but the audience has no need for explanation. There yet remains the problem of Caliban and his fellow-conspirators, whose bedraggled appearance does something to renew the sniping spirit of Sebastian and Antonio. Alonso's servants, the drunken butler and Trinculo the jester, are soon despatched, licking their wounds but largely undaunted by their recent experiences and their humiliating discovery. Caliban, however, seems to reach some kind of enlightenment:

> I'll be wise hereafter,
> And seek for grace. What a thrice-double ass
> Was I to take this drunkard for a god,
> And worship this dull fool!

Giving Ariel his final orders, Prospero parts not only from his 'chick' but from the whole world of spirits, releasing Ariel 'to the elements' and preparing himself for return to the everyday world of Milan.

Epilogue 'Please you draw near.' Prospero's final words were probably intended to invite the play's other human characters into the cell which had been his and Miranda's home for the past twelve years— but they could also be taken as an invitation to the audience to enter into a new and intimate relationship with Prospero himself. The former magician is now powerless: his staff is broken, his books are drowned, and Ariel has left him. Now *he* is the captive, and he must plead for his own release. Applause from the audience will break the magic spell, their words of praise would speed his departure, and their prayers would save him from the desperation which is all too often the fate of the dispossessed conjuror.

State of the art

... It is difficult to resist the conclusion that Shakespeare was getting bored with himself. Bored with people, bored with real life, bored, in fact, with everything except poetry and poetic dreams. He is no longer interested, one feels, in what happens, or who says what, so long as he can find place for a faultless lyric, or a new unimagined rhythmical effect, or a grand and mystic speech ...

That's what Lytton Strachey thought in 1906 when he was considering the group of four plays (*Pericles*, *Cymbeline*, *The Winter's Tale*, and *The Tempest*) written towards the end of Shakespeare's dramatic career. He was wrong! Nothing could be further from the truth.

Shakespeare was at the height of his powers. Behind him were almost twenty years in which his plays had dominated the London stage—comedies, histories, and the great tragedies, all suiting the mood of the period for which they were designed, and the resources of the companies who performed them. Living in a fast-changing age, Shakespeare moved with the times. He never stood still, never stopped learning, and was always *experimenting*. Now there was a new monarch, James I, and a new court, with different tastes in entertainment and different expectations from the theatre; there were new men—younger writers and critics who brought fresh ideas and influences to bear upon the stage; and there were innovations in theatrical design and technology. Shakespeare, far from being 'bored', was *challenged*—and he responded to the challenge not by following any of the trends exclusively, but by incorporating the latest fashions into a kind of drama that was uniquely his own.

The great delight at the court of King James was in the masque, a grand spectacular entertainment which combined song, speech, and dance in a display which was primarily visual in its appeal. Sometimes the designer and his elaborate scenery were more prominent than the writer! Intellectually the masque concerned itself most frequently with the attributes of kingship, seeming to instruct the royal patron but in fact exhibiting his virtues for the applause of his guests, often the representatives of foreign powers on official visitations. Those dramatists who devised masques rarely had any illusions about the value of what they were doing: masques, said Samuel Daniel, were '*punctilios* [i.e. trifles] of dreams and shows' created by 'poor engineers for shadows, [who] frame only images of no result'.[1] William Alexander was not the only poet to draw a comparison between the ephemerality of the masque and the mutability of human existence:

> Let greatness of her glassy sceptres vaunt;
> Not sceptres, no, but reeds, soon bruis'd, soon broken:
>   And let this worldly pomp our wits enchant,
> All fades, and scarcely leaves behind a token.
>
>   Those golden palaces, those gorgeous halls,
> With furniture superfluously fair;
>   Those stately courts, those sky-encount'ring walls
> Evanish all like vapours in the air.[2]

Apart from the betrothal-masque in *The Tempest*, Shakespeare, so far as we know, never attempted the form himself—unlike his contemporary, Ben Jonson, who wrote masques (of which he was exceedingly proud) as well as 'straight' plays. Both dramatists worked for the same company, the King's Men, and Shakespeare is known to have acted in plays written by his colleague. Jonson boasted a better classical education than Shakespeare, and took pains to make plays that conformed to the standards of the Greeks and Romans, especially in the matter of the 'three unities'. This met with the approval of the neoclassical critics of the period—and was in total contrast to Shakespeare's plays which, most of the time, cheerfully flouted all the 'rules'. *The Tempest*, however, is the exception—a model of correctness! As such it was highly commended by a much later theorist, the eighteenth-century scholar Joseph Warton, whose praise explains the 'unities' most succinctly:

> . . . the unities of action, of place, and of time, are in this play, though almost constantly violated by Shakespeare, exactly observed. The action is one, great, and entire: the restoration of Prospero to his dukedom; this business is transacted in the compass of a small island, and in or near the cave of Prospero

---

[1] *Vision of the Twelve Goddesses* (1605) and *Tethys' Festival* (1610).
[2] *Darius* by William Alexander (1603); compare *The Tempest*, 4, 1, 148–58.

(though, indeed, it had been more artful and regular to have confined it to this single spot); and the time which the action takes up is only equal to that of the representation—an excellence which ought always to be aimed at in every well-ordered fable . . .

(Joseph Warton, 'Remarks on the Creation of Character', 1753)

Even Ben Jonson could not have surpassed such 'regularity'—although he could find other faults in *The Tempest*. In his own play *Bartholomew Fair* (1614) he makes a mock-apology to the audience with a slighting but—perhaps—good-humoured reference to Shakespeare:

. . . If there be never a servant-monster i'the fair, who can help it? . . . nor a nest of antics? [The author] is loth to make nature afraid in his plays, like those that beget tales, tempests, and such-like drolleries.

(Induction, lines 127–30)

Another dramatist writing for the King's Men was John Fletcher, who collaborated with Shakespeare on such plays as *The Two Noble Kinsmen* and *Henry VIII* and who, after Shakespeare's death, became the leading dramatist for the company. Fletcher's favourite dramatic form was Italian tragicomedy, in which the dangerous action only *threatened* disaster and was finally resolved with a 'happy ever after' ending. Shakespeare responded to him with the 'romances'—including *The Tempest*—which are differentiated from Fletcherian tragicomedy mainly in the degree of seriousness with which the issues are treated.

In 1608 the King's Men acquired a new venue in the Blackfriars playhouse, an indoor theatre. There was seating for all the audience, with artificial lighting and even more sophisticated machinery for the stage. It was, of course, more expensive for the theatre-goers—and consequently drew a more élite audience. Shakespeare's plays continued to be performed at the open-air Globe theatre, but clearly he was thinking of the facilities and equipment of Blackfriars when he was writing the last 'romances'—and especially *The Tempest*. Here the airborne goddesses, flying harpy, and disappearing banquet all demand mechanical aid, whilst the break between Acts 4 and 5 seems intended to allow time for 'front of house' staff to replenish the candles and torches lighting the stage.

Shakespeare bored? Never!

Shakespeare's Verse

Shakespeare's plays are written mainly in blank verse, the form preferred by most dramatists in the sixteenth and early seventeenth centuries. It is a very flexible medium, capable—like the human speaking voice—of a wide range of tones. Basically, the lines, which are unrhymed, are ten syllables long. The syllables have alternating stresses, just like normal English speech, and they divide into five 'feet'. The technical name for this is 'iambic pentameter'. For *The Tempest* the rhythm is inaugurated by Miranda in the second scene of the play.

> **Miranda**
> If bý your árt, my déarest fáther, yóu have
> Put thé wild wáters ín this róar, alláy them.
> The ský, it séems, would póur down stínking pítch,
> But thát the séa, mountíng to th' wélkin's chéek,
> Dashés the fire out. Ó, I háve sufférd'd
> With thóse that Í saw súffer: á brave véssel—
> Who hád, no doúbt, some nóble créatures ín her—
> Dash'd áll to piéces! Ó, the crý did knóck
> Agáinst my véry héart—poor sóuls, they pérish'd.
> Had Í been ány gód of pówer, I wóuld
> Have súnk the séa withín the éarth or ére
> It shóuld the góod ship só have swállow'd, ánd
> The fráughting sóuls withín her.

Miranda's grief is almost as wild as the raging sea that she describes, but the lines in which it is uttered are mostly regular pentameters with, usually, a mid-line break (a 'caesura') which allows for added emphasis and greater control. The little speech builds to a climax of passion which has to be restrained by her father, who shares the verse line with her:

> **Prospero**
>   Bé colléct'd.
> No móre amázement. Téll your píteous heart
> There's nó harm dóne.

Miranda
> O, wóe the dáy!

Prospero
>   No hárm.
> I háve done nóthing bút in cáre of thée,
> Of thée, my déar one, thée, my dáughter . . .

At the beginning of his career, Shakespeare wrote verse whose lines were mainly 'end-stopped', and where the grammatical unit of meaning was contained within each pentameter—as in Miranda's question 'What fóul play hád we thát we cáme from thénce?' (line 60). End-stopped lines are rare in *The Tempest*. Shakespeare is completely in command of every aspect of his medium, and the flexibility of his verse, in which the sense often runs effortlessly between the lines, allows the characters to express their intimate feelings, private hopes and fears, easy jokes and formal warnings, speaking either to each other or else '*aside*' to the audience.

A line can be shared between different speakers without losing its rhythm; as in everyday speech, syllables may be elided ('o'th' ', 't' advance'); and occasionally an incomplete pentameter speaks more than words can articulate: 'By providence divine' (*1*, 2, 159).

Source

The Tempest has many sources—and yet no source at all! There is no counterpart, either in fact or in fiction, for the plot of Prospero's revenge on the brother whose political coup had usurped his state—but there is much, in life and in literature, that can account for part of the action, most of the human characters, a few of the ideas, and even some of the verse.

A particular incident, the wreck of the *Sea-Adventure* in 1609, gave the play's starting-point, and the *dramatis personae* of Shakespeare's earlier plays are, very often, the immediate ancestors of the characters of *The Tempest* (although their roots go much deeper). Certain passages from the *Essays* of Montaigne gave Shakespeare food for thought, and he found inspiration for Prospero's final invocation of his spirits in the words of the witch Medea in Ovid's *Metamorphoses*. Other echoes resonate throughout the play, most especially those of Virgil's *Aeneid*. This provided Shakespeare with the vanishing banquet, the lecture of the harpy, and also, with other minor details, the pointless and mirthless jesting of Antonio and Sebastian about 'widow Dido' and 'widower Aeneas'.

Quite a different kind of influence was Shakespeare's own verse. On several occasions he reverts to images and ideas that recall, perhaps intentionally, his earlier plays, re-working them for his present purpose. The 'sea-change' described in Ariel's song (*1*, 2, 397–405) has its origins in the dream-vision of Clarence in *Richard III*; Ferdinand's praise of Miranda (*3*, 1, 46–8) recapitulates and summarizes the praises of Orlando for Rosalind in *As You Like It*; and Ferdinand later (*4*, 1, 30–1) adopts Juliet's imagery to express eager anticipation of the wedding-night.

Date

The Tempest was performed at court 'before the King's Majesty' on 1 November 1611. Although this was not necessarily the first performance, it must have been an early one, since Shakespeare, indebted to Strachey's letter for details of the shipwreck, could not have started writing the play before the letter, dated Virginia 15 July 1610, reached England—probably in September of that year.

Text

The play was first published in the Folio of 1623. It is the very first play in that volume, and the text is remarkable for its careful presentation: there are few obvious corruptions, some very careful punctuation, complete act and scene division, and unusually elaborate stage directions. The theatrical manuscript must have been specially transcribed for a reading public, perhaps because the publishers had a particular respect for *The Tempest*—or perhaps because they wanted to impress potential buyers with the quality of their book.

Characters in the Play

ON BOARD THE SHIP

Alonso *King of Naples*

Sebastian *his brother*

Ferdinand *his son*

Antonio *his brother, usurping Duke of Milan*

Gonzalo *an honest old councillor*

Adrian

lords

Francisco

Trinculo *a jester*

Stephano *a drunken butler*

Master *of the king's ship*

Boatswain

Mariners

ON THE ISLAND

Prospero   *the rightful Duke of Milan*

Miranda   *his daughter*

Ariel   *an airy spirit*

Caliban   *a savage and deformed slave*

Iris   *messenger of the gods*

Ceres   *goddess of fertility*   } *personated by spirits*

Juno   *queen of the gods*

Spirits personating Nymphs and Reapers

After the first scene on board a ship at sea, the action takes place in different parts of a desert island

Act 1

Act 1   Scene 1

In a violent storm the sailors are wrestling
with masts and sails to control their ship—
whose passengers, the King of Naples and
his courtiers, are adding to the confusion of
the tempest.

3 *Good*: A comment, not an answer:
'Good man', 'Good, you're here'; *not*
'Good cheer'.
Fall to't yarely: get on with it smartly.

5 *Cheerly*: Cheerily, with a good will.
6 *Tend*: pay attention.
7 *whistle*: On board ship, sailors are given
instructions by blasts on the boatswain's
whistle.
Blow . . . wind: blow as hard as you like.
8 *if room enough*: so long as there is open
sea (i.e. with no rocks or sandbanks).

10 *Play the men*: be good chaps now.

12 *bos'n*: bosun, the usual pronunciation of
'boatswain'.

Scene 1

*A tempestuous noise of thunder and lightning
heard. Enter a* Ship-master *and a* Boatswain

Master
Boatswain!
Boatswain
Here, master. What cheer?
Master
Good—speak to th' mariners. Fall to't yarely, or we
run ourselves aground. Bestir, bestir!   [*Exit*

Enter Mariners

Boatswain
5 Hey, my hearts! Cheerly, cheerly, my hearts! Yare,
yare! Take in the topsail. Tend to th' master's
whistle. [*To the storm*]—Blow till thou burst thy
wind, if room enough!

Enter Alonso, Sebastian, Antonio,
Ferdinand, Gonzalo, *and* others

Alonso
Good boatswain, have care. Where's the master?
10 [*To the* Mariners] Play the men.
Boatswain
I pray now, keep below.
Antonio
Where is the master, bos'n?
Boatswain
Do you not hear him? You mar our labour. Keep
your cabins—you do assist the storm.
Gonzalo
15 Nay, good, be patient.

16   *roarers*: rioters, i.e. the roaring winds
      and waters.

Boatswain

When the sea is. Hence! What cares these roarers for
the name of king? To cabin; silence! Trouble us not.

Gonzalo

Good, yet remember whom thou hast aboard.

Boatswain

None that I love more than myself. You are a
20 councillor; if you can command these elements to
silence, and work the peace of the present, we will
not hand a rope more—use your authority. If you
cannot, give thanks you have lived so long, and make
yourself ready in your cabin for the mischance of the
25 hour, if it so hap. [*To the* Mariners]—Cheerly, good
hearts! [*To the* courtiers]—Out of our way, I say!
                                          [*Exit*

23–4 *make yourself ready*: prepare yourself,
      physically and spiritually.

25   *hap*: happen, chance.

Gonzalo

I have great comfort from this fellow. Methinks he
hath no drowning mark upon him—his complexion
is perfect gallows. Stand fast, good Fate, to his
30 hanging, make the rope of his destiny our cable, for
our own doth little advantage. If he be not born to be
hanged, our case is miserable.
                                          [*Exeunt*

Enter Boatswain

27–9 *he hath . . . gallows*: Gonzalo refers to
      a proverb 'he that is born to be hanged
      shall never be drowned'.

28   *complexion*: appearance, i.e. character as
      seen in the face.

29   *Stand fast*: keep true.

30   *his destiny*: for which he is destined.

31   *doth little advantage*: is not much use to
      us.

Boatswain

Down with the topmast! Yare! Lower, lower! Bring
her to try with main-course. [*A cry within*] A plague
35 upon this howling! They are louder than the weather
or our office.

Enter Sebastian, Antonio, *and* Gonzalo

Yet again? What do you here? Shall we give o'er and
drown? Have you a mind to sink?

Sebastian

A pox o' your throat, you bawling, blasphemous,
40 incharitable dog!

Boatswain

Work you, then.

Antonio

Hang, cur, hang, you whoreson insolent noisemaker!
We are less afraid to be drowned than thou art.

33–48 *Down with . . . lay her off*: The storm
      is blowing the ship on to the rocks, and
      the sailors must lower the mast to
      reduce the weight aloft, keep close to
      the wind, and try to sail out to open
      sea.

34   *try with main-course*: To 'try' was to
      lower the mainsail and keep as close to
      the wind as possible.

35   *They*: i.e. the passengers.

36   *office*: us at our work.

38   *a mind to*: a wish to.

39–40 *A pox . . . dog*: Sebastian's abuse
      seems unwarranted—unless something
      has been omitted or censored from the
      text.

44 *for*: against; Gonzalo repeats his joke of lines 27–9.

46 *unstanched wench*: girl whose bleeding is unstopped.

47 *Lay her a-hold*: bring a ship close to the wind so as to hold it steady: to do this requires more sail—hence the next order.
courses: sails.

50 *must . . . cold*: 'cold in the mouth (= dead)' was a proverbial phrase; perhaps the Boatswain also takes a swig from a bottle, provoking Antonio's anger still further.

52 *case*: situation.

53 *merely*: simply, completely.

54 *wide-chopped*: big-mouthed.
would: I wish.

54–5 *would . . . tides*: The usual punishment for pirates was to be left hanging at the low water mark until three tides had washed over them.

57 *glut*: swallow, engulf.

64 *brown furze*: heather and gorse.

65 *The wills above*: i.e. God's will.
fain: like to.

Gonzalo

I'll warrant him for drowning, though the ship were
45 no stronger than a nutshell and as leaky as an
unstanched wench.

Boatswain

Lay her a-hold, a-hold! Set her two courses off to sea
again; lay her off!

Enter Mariners *wet*

Mariners

All lost! To prayers, to prayers! All lost!   [*Exeunt*

Boatswain

50 What, must our mouths be cold?

Gonzalo

The king and prince at prayers, let's assist them,
For our case is as theirs.

Sebastian

                    I'm out of patience.

Antonio

We are merely cheated of our lives by drunkards.
This wide-chopped rascal—would thou mightst lie
drowning
55 The washing of ten tides!   [*Exit* Boatswain

Gonzalo

                    He'll be hanged yet,
Though every drop of water swear against it,
And gape at wid'st to glut him.

A confused noise within

'Mercy on us!'—'We split, we split!'—
'Farewell, my wife and children!'—'Farewell,
60 brother!'—'We split! we split! we split!'

Antonio

Let's all sink wi' th' king.

Sebastian

Let's take leave of him.   [*Exit with* Antonio

Gonzalo

Now would I give a thousand furlongs of sea for an
acre of barren ground—long heath, brown furze,
65 anything. The wills above be done, but I would fain
die a dry death.   [*Exit*

Act 1   Scene 2

This long scene, introducing all the major characters and themes of the play, sets the action in motion. First Prospero tells Miranda (and the audience) how they were expelled from Milan through the treachery of his brother, reaching the safety of this island only by the mercy of providence—which has now enabled him, with his magic powers, to raise the storm that we have just witnessed. Prospero's two servants, Ariel and Caliban, are individually presented: Ariel recounts his activities in the shipwreck, and Caliban grumbles about his servitude. Ferdinand, led by the charm of music, is brought in by Ariel. He immediately falls in love with Miranda, and she with him.

  1 *art*: magic power.
  3 *pitch*: black tar.
  4 *welkin's cheek*: face of heaven.
  5 *fire*: lightning (imagined as the fire that boils the pitch).
  6 *brave*: splendid.
10 *god of power*: Only the most powerful gods could command the storms.
11 *or ere*: before.
13 *fraughting*: being carried as freight.
14 *amazement*: fearful bewilderment.
    piteous: pitying.

Scene 2

The island. Enter Prospero *and* Miranda

Miranda
If by your art, my dearest father, you have
Put the wild waters in this roar, allay them.
The sky, it seems, would pour down stinking pitch,
But that the sea, mounting to th' welkin's cheek,
5 Dashes the fire out. O, I have suffer'd
With those that I saw suffer: a brave vessel—
Who had, no doubt, some noble creature in her—
Dash'd all to pieces! O, the cry did knock
Against my very heart—poor souls, they perish'd.
10 Had I been any god of power, I would
Have sunk the sea within the earth or ere
It should the good ship so have swallow'd, and
The fraughting souls within her.
    Prospero
                               Be collected.
No more amazement. Tell your piteous heart
15 There's no harm done.

Miranda
                                        O, woe the day!

Prospero
                                                No harm.
I have done nothing but in care of thee,
Of thee, my dear one, thee, my daughter, who
Art ignorant of what thou art; naught knowing
Of whence I am, nor that I am more better
20 Than Prospero, master of a full poor cell,
And thy no greater father.

Miranda
                                        More to know
Did never meddle with my thoughts.

Prospero
                                                'Tis time
I should inform thee farther. Lend thy hand
And pluck my magic garment from me.

                Miranda helps him to disrobe

                                                So.
25 Lie there, my art.—Wipe thou thine eyes; have
        comfort.
The direful spectacle of the wreck, which touch'd
The very virtue of compassion in thee,
I have with such provision in mine art
So safely order'd that there is no soul,
30 No, not so much perdition as an hair
Betid to any creature in the vessel
Which thou heard'st cry, which thou saw'st sink. Sit
        down,
For thou must now know farther.

                        They sit

Miranda
                                        You have often
Begun to tell me what I am, but stopp'd,
35 And left me to a bootless inquisition,
Concluding, 'Stay, not yet.'

Prospero
                                        The hour's now come;
The very minute bids thee ope thine ear.
Obey, and be attentive. Canst thou remember
A time before we came unto this cell?

---

19 *more better*: of any higher rank.
20 *full*: very.
    cell: dwelling, cottage.

22 *meddle with*: enter into.

24 *magic garment*: i.e. the magician's robe.

25 *my art*: Cloak, wand, and book are essential requirements for Prospero's conjuring.
26 *spectacle*: The word usually refers to a theatrical display or pageant.

30 *perdition*: loss.
31 *Betid*: befell, happened to.

35 *bootless*: unsuccessful.
    inquisition: questioning, enquiry.

41 *Out*: more than.

42 *By what*: i.e. by what recollection.
43–4 *Of anything . . . remembrance*: describe to me whatever it is that you can remember.

46 *warrants*: guarantees.
47 *tended*: looked after.

50 *backward . . . time*: the depths of the past.

54 *Milan*: The word is stressed on the first syllable.

56 *piece*: model.

59 *no worse issued*: no less noble in descent.

61 *Or . . . we did*: or was it fortunate that we did [come away].

63 *holp*: helped.

40 I do not think thou canst, for then thou wast not
Out three years old.
Miranda
                       Certainly, sir, I can.
Prospero
By what? By any other house or person?
Of anything the image tell me that
Hath kept with thy remembrance.
Miranda
                            'Tis far off,
45 And rather like a dream than an assurance
That my remembrance warrants. Had I not
Four or five women once that tended me?
Prospero
Thou hadst, and more, Miranda; but how is it
That this lives in thy mind? What seest thou else
50 In the dark backward and abyss of time?
If thou rememb'rest aught ere thou cam'st here,
How thou cam'st here thou mayst.
Miranda
                          But that I do not.
Prospero
Twelve year since, Miranda, twelve year since,
Thy father was the Duke of Milan, and
55 A prince of power—
Miranda
                    Sir, are you not my father?
Prospero
Thy mother was a piece of virtue, and
She said thou wast my daughter; and thy father
Was Duke of Milan, and his only heir
And princess no worse issued.
Miranda
                        O, the heavens!
60 What foul play had we that we came from thence?
Or blessed was't we did?
Prospero
                  Both, both, my girl.
By foul play, as thou sayst, were we heav'd thence,
But blessedly holp hither.
Miranda
                    O, my heart bleeds

64 *teen*: trouble.
65 *from*: not present in.

70 *manage*: administration.
71 *signories*: dukedoms (a description particularly applied to the Italian city-states).
73 *liberal arts*: scholarship, especially the subjects considered suitable studies for a gentleman, making up the *trivium* (grammar, logic, and rhetoric) and the *quadrivium* (arithmetic, geometry, music, and astronomy).
76 *transported*: carried away.
77 *rapt*: engrossed.
    secret studies: i.e. the study of magic.

79 *perfected*: completely versed in (the word is stressed on the first and third syllables).
    suits: requests.
80 *advance*: promote.
81 *trash*: hold back, leash in (like a greyhound).
    overtopping: growing too high, getting too much power.
82 *creatures that were mine*: ministers whom I had appointed to office.
82–3 *or changed . . . 'em*: either replaced them or changed their responsibilities.
83–4 *both . . . office*: control over both ministers and administration.
83 *key*: The office key has now become the key of musical notation.
85 *what*: whatever.
    that: so that.

To think o'th' teen that I have turn'd you to,
65 Which is from my remembrance. Please you, farther.
    Prospero
    My brother, and thy uncle, call'd Antonio—
    I pray thee mark me, that a brother should
    Be so perfidious—he whom next thyself
    Of all the world I lov'd, and to him put
70 The manage of my state, as at that time
    Through all the signories it was the first,
    And Prospero the prime duke, being so reputed
    In dignity, and for the liberal arts
    Without a parallel; those being all my study,
75 The government I cast upon my brother,
    And to my state grew stranger, being transported
    And rapt in secret studies. Thy false uncle—
    Dost thou attend me?
    Miranda
                            Sir, most heedfully.
    Prospero
    Being once perfected how to grant suits,
80 How to deny them, who t'advance, and who
    To trash for overtopping, new created
    The creatures that were mine, I say: or chang'd 'em,
    Or else new form'd 'em; having both the key
    Of officer and office, set all hearts i'th' state
85 To what tune pleas'd his ear, that now he was

The ivy which had hid my princely trunk,
And suck'd my verdure out on't—thou attend'st not!

86 *trunk*: Prospero envisages himself as a tree.
87 *verdure*: sap, vitality—hence, power.

90 *closeness*: privacy.
91–2 *but . . . rate*: was beyond the understanding of most people simply because it was private.
94 *Like a good parent*: Prospero alludes to the proverb, 'Great men's sons seldom do well'.
beget: Prospero seems to take responsibility for the 'falsehood' of his brother.
97 *sans*: without.
lorded: turned into a lord.
98 *revenue*: income; the word is stressed on the second syllable.
100–2 *having . . . lie*: having told this lie so often, he made his own memory commit such sin against truth as to credit it.
103 *out o'th' substitution*: as a consequence of having taken my place.
104–5 *executing . . . prerogative*: officiating with every appearance and privilege of royalty.

Miranda
O, good sir, I do!
　　　Prospero
　　　　　　　　I pray thee mark me:
　　I thus neglecting worldly ends, all dedicated
90　To closeness and the bettering of my mind
　　With that which, but by being so retir'd,
　　O'er-priz'd all popular rate, in my false brother
　　Awak'd an evil nature, and my trust,
　　Like a good parent, did beget of him
95　A falsehood in its contrary as great
　　As my trust was, which had, indeed, no limit,
　　A confidence sans bound. He being thus lorded,
　　Not only with what my revenue yielded,
　　But what my power might else exact, like one
100　Who, having into truth by telling of it,
　　Made such a sinner of his memory
　　To credit his own lie, he did believe
　　He was indeed the duke, out o'th' substitution
　　And executing th'outward face of royalty

105 With all prerogative. Hence his ambition growing—
Dost thou hear?

Miranda
                              Your tale, sir, would cure deafness.

Prospero
To have no screen between this part he play'd
And him he play'd it for, he needs will be
Absolute Milan. Me, poor man, my library
110 Was dukedom large enough. Of temporal royalties
He thinks me now incapable; confederates—
So dry he was for sway—with' King of Naples
To give him annual tribute, do him homage,
Subject his coronet to his crown, and bend
115 The dukedom yet unbow'd—alas, poor Milan!—
To most ignoble stooping.

Miranda
                              O, the heavens!

Prospero
Mark his condition, and th'event; then tell me
If this might be a brother.

Miranda
                              I should sin
To think but nobly of my grandmother:
120 Good wombs have borne bad sons.

Prospero
                              Now the condition.
This King of Naples, being an enemy
To me inveterate, hearkens my brother's suit,
Which was that he, in lieu o'th' premises
Of homage and I know not how much tribute,
125 Should presently extirpate me and mine
Out of the dukedom, and confer fair Milan,
With all the honours, on my brother; whereon,
A treacherous army levied, one midnight
Fated to th' purpose did Antonio open
130 The gates of Milan, and i'th' dead of darkness
The ministers for th' purpose hurried thence
Me and thy crying self.

Miranda
                              Alack, for pity!
I not rememb'ring how I cried out then
Will cry it o'er again—it is a hint
135 That wrings mine eyes to't.

107–8 *To have . . . played it for*: so that there would be no separation between the role (i.e. Duke of Milan) and the man on whose behalf it was performed.

108–9 *he needs . . . Milan*: he must become himself the Duke of Milan.

110 *large*: spacious.

110–11 *Of temporal . . . incapable*: he thinks me no longer competent to govern worldly affairs; Prospero, his verbs all in the present tense, re-lives the experience he is describing.

111 *confederates*: conspires.

112 *dry*: thirsty, eager.
sway: power.

113 *him*: i.e. to the King of Naples.

115 *yet unbow'd*: hitherto independent.

117 *his condition . . . event*: the terms of his agreement with the King of Naples and the outcome.

123 *in lieu . . . premises*: in return for the conditions agreed upon.

125 *presently*: immediately.
extirpate: eradicate, wipe out.

128 *levied*: having been levied.

129 *Fated*: appointed by Fate.

131 *ministers*: agents.

134 *hint*: occasion.

135 *wrings*: wrings tears from.
to't: about it.

Prospero

                    Hear a little further,
And then I'll bring thee to the present business
Which now's upon 's; without the which this story
Were most impertinent.

Miranda

                  Wherefore did they not
That hour destroy us?

Prospero

                 Well demanded, wench:
140 My tale provokes that question. Dear, they durst not,
So dear the love my people bore me, nor set
A mark so bloody on the business; but
With colours fairer painted their foul ends.
In few, they hurried us aboard a barque,
145 Bore us some leagues to sea, where they prepar'd
A rotten carcass of a butt, not rigg'd,
Nor tackle, sail, nor mast—the very rats
Instinctively have quit it. There they hoist us
To cry to th' sea that roar'd to us, to sigh
150 To th' winds, whose pity, sighing back again,
Did us but loving wrong.

137 *without the which*: i.e. without the 'present business'.
138 *impertinent*: irrelevant.

139 *wench*: lass (used as a term of endearment).
140 *durst*: dare.

143 *colours*: excuses.
144 *In few*: briefly.
barque: vessel—although Milan is not a sea-port.
146 *carcass of a butt*: skeleton of a boat.
rigg'd: fitted out.
147 *tackle*: ropes.

Miranda
                                        Alack, what trouble
Was I then to you!
    Prospero
                                        O, a cherubin
Thou wast that did preserve me. Thou didst smile,
Infused with a fortitude from heaven,
155 When I have deck'd the sea with drops full salt,
Under my burden groan'd, which rais'd in me
An undergoing stomach to bear up
Against what should ensue.
    Miranda
                                        How came we ashore?
    Prospero
By providence divine;
160 Some food we had, and some fresh water, that
A noble Neapolitan, Gonzalo,
Out of his charity, who being then appointed
Master of this design, did give us, with
Rich garments, linens, stuffs, and necessaries,
165 Which since have steaded much; so of his gentleness,
Knowing I lov'd my books, he furnish'd me
From mine own library with volumes that
I prize above my dukedom.
    Miranda
                                        Would I might
But ever see that man!
    Prospero
[*Rising*]   Now I arise.
170 Sit still, and hear the last of our sea-sorrow:
Here in this island we arriv'd, and here
Have I, thy schoolmaster, made thee more profit
Than other princes can that have more time
For vainer hours, and tutors not so careful.
    Miranda
175 Heavens thank you for't. And now I pray you, sir,
For still 'tis beating in my mind, your reason
For raising this sea-storm.
    Prospero
                                        Know thus far forth:
By accident most strange, bountiful Fortune,
Now my dear lady, hath mine enemies

155 *deck'd*: decorated, adorned.
    full: very, exceedingly.
156–7 *Under . . . bear up*: In his choice of
    images, Prospero seems to identify his
    experience with that of a woman in
    childbirth.
157 *undergoing stomach*: courage to endure.

159 *By providence divine*: The metrically
    incomplete line allows a slight dramatic
    pause: Prospero gives Miranda both
    answer and explanation.
164 *stuffs*: household equipment.
165 *steaded much*: been very useful.
    gentleness: noble kindliness.
170 *Sit still*: remain seated.
172 *profit*: learn, get a better education.
173 *princes*: royal children.
174 *vainer hours*: leisure activities.
    careful: taking trouble, *and*, caring.
178 *Fortune*: Pictorial representations show a
    blind goddess, controlling the wheel of
    Fate and distributing favours at
    random.

180 *prescience*: foreknowledge.
181 *zenith*: highest point (of Fortune's wheel).
182 *influence*: astrological power.
183 *omit*: neglect, disregard.

185 *dulness*: drowsiness.

193 *quality*: colleagues.

194 *to point*: in every detail.

195 *article*: item (the term is legalistic).
196 *beak*: prow.
197 *in the waist*: amidships.
    deck: poop; early ships had only a small deck in the stern of the vessel.
198 *flam'd amazement*: caused bewilderment by appearing as a flickering flame; early navigators describe such phenomena, often referred to as 'St Elmo's fire' and usually taken as a good omen.
200 *yards*: yard-arms.
    flame distinctly: burn as separate flames.
202 *momentary*: instantaneous.
203 *sight-outrunning*: quicker than sight.
204 *sulphurous*: Sulphur became associated with thunder through its common use in gunpowder and explosives.

180 Brought to this shore; and by my prescience
I find my zenith doth depend upon
A most auspicious star, whose influence
If now I court not, but omit, my fortunes
Will ever after droop. Here cease more questions:
185 Thou art inclin'd to sleep. 'Tis a good dulness,
And give it way—I know thou canst not choose.

Miranda sleeps

[*Calling*] Come away, servant, come.

      [*Puts on his cloak*]   I am ready now.

Approach, my Ariel. Come.

Enter Ariel

Ariel
All hail, great master, grave sir, hail! I come
190 To answer thy best pleasure, be't to fly,
To swim, to dive into the fire, to ride
On the curl'd clouds; to thy strong bidding task
Ariel and all his quality.
Prospero
                Hast thou, spirit,
Perform'd to point the tempest that I bade thee?
Ariel
195 To every article.
I boarded the king's ship; now on the beak,
Now in the waist, the deck, in every cabin,
I flam'd amazement. Sometime I'd divide
And burn in many places; on the topmast,
200 The yards and bowsprit would I flame distinctly,
Then meet and join. Jove's lightning, the precursors
O'th' dreadful thunder-claps, more momentary
And sight-outrunning were not; the fire and cracks
Of sulphurous roaring the most mighty Neptune
205 Seem to besiege and make his bold waves tremble,
Yea, his dread trident shake.

Prospero
                                        My brave spirit!
Who was so firm, so constant, that this coil
Would not infect his reason?
          Ariel
                              Not a soul
But felt a fever of the mad, and play'd
210 Some tricks of desperation. All but mariners
Plung'd in the foaming brine and quit the vessel,
Then all afire with me: the king's son Ferdinand,
With hair up-staring—then like reeds, not hair—
Was the first man that leapt, cried 'Hell is empty,
215 And all the devils are here.'
          Prospero
                                        Why, that's my spirit.
But was not this nigh shore?
          Ariel
                                        Close by, my master.
          Prospero
But are they, Ariel, safe?

207 *constant*: level-headed.
    coil: disturbance, confusion.

209 *of the mad*: such as a madman might
    feel.

213 *up-staring*: standing on end.

Ariel
                                    Not a hair perish'd.
On their sustaining garments not a blemish,
But fresher than before; and as thou bad'st me,
220 In troops I have dispers'd them 'bout the isle.
The king's son have I landed by himself,
Whom I left cooling of the air with sighs
In an odd angle of the isle, and sitting,
His arms in this sad knot.
    Prospero
                            Of the king's ship
225 The mariners say how thou hast dispos'd,
And all the rest o'th' fleet.
    Ariel
                            Safely in harbour
Is the king's ship, in the deep nook where once
Thou called'st me up at midnight to fetch dew
From the still-vex'd Bermudas, there she's hid;
230 The mariners all under hatches stow'd,
Who, with a charm join'd to their suffer'd labour,
I have left asleep; and for the rest o'th' fleet,
Which I dispers'd, they all have met again,
And are upon the Mediterranean float,
235 Bound sadly home for Naples,
Supposing that they saw the king's ship wreck'd,
And his great person perish.
    Prospero
                                Ariel, thy charge
Exactly is perform'd; but there's more work.
What is the time o'th' day?
    Ariel
                            Past the mid-season.
    Prospero
240 At least two glasses. The time 'twixt six and now
Must by us both be spent most preciously.
    Ariel
Is there more toil? Since thou dost give me pains,
Let me remember thee what thou hast promis'd,
Which is not yet perform'd me.
    Prospero
                                How now? Moody?
245 What is't thou canst demand?

218 *sustaining garments*: Their clothes somehow (perhaps by Ariel's magic) buoyed them up in the water.
220 *troops*: groups.

223 *angle*: corner.
224 *this sad knot*: folded across his chest.

229 *still-vex'd Bermudas*: The Bermudas were popularly supposed to be troubled with many storms.
230 *under hatches*: below deck.
231 *Who*: whom.
    their suffer'd labour: the labour they have endured.
234 *float*: sea.

240 *two glasses*: two hour-glasses; i.e. two hours past noon.

242 *pains*: tasks.
243 *remember*: remind.
244 *me*: for me.

Ariel
My liberty.

Prospero
Before the time be out? No more.

246 *out*: expired.

Ariel
I prithee,
Remember I have done thee worthy service,
Told thee no lies, made no mistakings, serv'd
Without or grudge or grumblings. Thou did promise
250 To bate me a full year.

249 *or . . . or*: either . . . or.
250 *bate me*: reduce my time by, knock off.

Prospero
Dost thou forget
From what a torment I did free thee?

Ariel
No.

Prospero
Thou dost, and think'st it much to tread the ooze
Of the salt deep,
To run upon the sharp wind of the north,
255 To do me business in the veins o'th' earth
When it is baked with frost.

252 *much*: too much.

255 *veins o'th' earth*: mineral deposits, *or*, underground streams.

Ariel
I do not, sir.

Prospero
Thou liest, malignant thing! Hast thou forgot
The foul witch Sycorax, who with age and envy
Was grown into a hoop? Hast thou forgot her?

Ariel
260 No, sir.

Prospero
Thou hast. Where was she born? Speak; tell me.

Ariel
Sir, in Algiers.

Prospero
O, was she so—I must
Once in a month recount what thou hast been,
Which thou forget'st. This damn'd witch Sycorax,
For mischiefs manifold and sorceries terrible
265 To enter human hearing, from Algiers
Thou know'st was banish'd—for one thing she did
They would not take her life. Is not this true?

261 *was she so*: so you do remember.

266 *one thing she did*: This deed is never explained or ever mentioned again; it may have been because the witch was pregnant.

Ariel

Ay, sir.

Prospero

This blue-eyed hag was hither brought with child,

270 And here was left by th' sailors. Thou, my slave,

As thou report'st thyself, was then her servant,

And for thou wast a spirit too delicate

To act her earthy and abhorred commands,

Refusing her grand hests, she did confine thee,

275 By help of her more potent ministers

And in her most unmitigable rage,

Into a cloven pine, within which rift

Imprison'd thou didst painfully remain

A dozen years; within which space she died

280 And left thee there, where thou didst vent thy groans

As fast as mill-wheels strike. Then was this island—

Save for the son that she did litter here,

A freckled whelp, hag-born—not honour'd with

A human shape.

Ariel

                    Yes, Caliban, her son.

Prospero

285 Dull thing, I say so: he, that Caliban

Whom now I keep in service. Thou best know'st

What torment I did find thee in. Thy groans

269 *blue-eyed*: A blueish shadow on the eyelids was thought to be a sign of pregnancy.

273 *earthy*: sordid; being 'of the earth', they would be particularly antipathetic to Ariel's nature.

274 *hests*: behests, commands.

280 *vent*: utter.

281 *mill-wheels*: i.e. the blades of waterwheels.

285 *Dull thing*: Prospero resents the interruption—which is, however, needful for the understanding of the audience.

288 *breasts*: hearts.

Did make wolves howl, and penetrate the breasts
Of ever-angry bears—it was a torment
290 To lay upon the damn'd, which Sycorax
Could not again undo. It was mine art,
When I arrived and heard thee, that made gape
The pine and let thee out.

291 *It was mine art*: Prospero's magic succeeded where the witch's power had failed (and when Sycorax was dead).

   Ariel
           I thank thee, master.

   Prospero
If thou more murmur'st, I will rend an oak
295 And peg thee in his knotty entrails till
Thou hast howl'd away twelve winters.

   Ariel
            Pardon, master.

297 *correspondent*: responsive.
298 *do . . . gently*: be a docile spirit.

I will be correspondent to command
And do my spriting gently.

   Prospero
        Do so, and after two days
I will discharge thee.

   Ariel
        That's my noble master.
300 What shall I do? Say what: what shall I do?

   Prospero
Go, make thyself like a nymph o'th'sea.
Be subject to no sight but thine and mine, invisible
To every eyeball else. Go, take this shape,
And hither come in't; go! Hence, with diligence!

             [Exit Ariel

301–4 *Go . . . in't*: This disguise (like Ariel's interjection at line 284) must be for the benefit of the audience; there would be little point in it if the spirit is to be invisible except to Prospero. Some editors, however, suggest that there has been interference with Shakespeare's text.

305 [*To* Miranda] Awake, dear heart, awake. Thou hast
  slept well.
Awake.

   Miranda
     The strangeness of your story put
Heaviness in me.

307 *Heaviness*: drowsiness.

   Prospero
         Shake it off. Come on;
We'll visit Caliban, my slave, who never
Yields us kind answer.

   Miranda
        'Tis a villain, sir,
310 I do not love to look on.

Prospero

> But as 'tis,
> We cannot miss him. He does make our fire,
> Fetch in our wood, and serves in offices
> That profit us. What ho, slave! Caliban!
> Thou earth, thou, speak!

Caliban

[*Within*]   There's wood enough within.

Prospero

315 Come forth, I say; there's other business for thee.
> Come, thou tortoise, when?

Enter Ariel *like a water-nymph*

> Fine apparition! My quaint Ariel,
> Hark in thine ear. [*Whispers*]

Ariel

> My lord, it shall be done.   [*Exit*

Prospero

> Thou poisonous slave, got by the devil himself
320 Upon thy wicked dam, come forth!

Enter Caliban

Caliban

> As wicked dew as e'er my mother brush'd
> With raven's feather from unwholesome fen
> Drop on you both! A south-west blow on ye
> And blister you all o'er!

Prospero

325 For this be sure tonight thou shalt have cramps,
> Side-stitches that shall pen thy breath up. Urchins
> Shall, for that vast of night that they may work,
> All exercise on thee. Thou shalt be pinch'd
> As thick as honeycomb, each pinch more stinging
330 Than bees that made 'em.

Caliban

> I must eat my dinner.
> This island's mine by Sycorax my mother,
> Which thou tak'st from me. When thou cam'st first
> Thou strok'st me and made much of me; wouldst give me
> Water with berries in't, and teach me how
335 To name the bigger light and how the less,
> That burn by day and night; and then I lov'd thee,

---

311 *miss*: do without.

314 *earth*: Caliban is contrasted with Ariel, the spirit of air, fire, and water.

314s.d. *Within*: i.e. offstage; Caliban is perhaps in the 'discovery space', a curtained area at the back of the stage (which is also used at 5, 1, 171).

316 *tortoise*: The epithet might have been prompted by a reference in the Strachey letter to edible tortoise found by the colonists shipwrecked on the Bermudas (see 'Shakespeare's Sources', p. 89). *when?*: Prospero is impatient.

317 *quaint*: ingenious, exquisite.

319 *got*: begotten: witches were often accused of having sexual intercourse with the devil.

321 *wicked dew*: Morning dew was thought to be unhealthy, and often used in magical potions.

322 *raven*: The bird was often associated with witchcraft—and its Greek name—*korax*—must have been used in the formation of the name 'Sycorax'.

323 *south-west*: This wind, bringing warm damp weather, was considered unwholesome.

326 *Urchins*: hedgehogs, goblins (who often assumed the form of hedgehogs).

327 *vast*: great extent.

328–30 *pinched . . . made 'em*: covered with sharp pinches all over as though you were a honeycomb (the wax of whose cells, it was thought, was moulded by being pinched into shape by the bees).

331 *by Sycorax my mother*: Caliban bases his claim to ownership of the island on inheritance.

335 *bigger . . . less*: The phraseology is that of the Bible: 'God then made two great lights; the greater light to rule the day, and the less light to rule the night' (Genesis 47: 3).

And show'd thee all the qualities o'th' isle,
The fresh springs, brine pits, barren place and
    fertile—

339 *charms*: spells.

Curs'd be I that did so! All the charms
340 Of Sycorax, toads, beetles, bats light on you!
For I am all the subjects that you have,
Which first was mine own king, and here you sty
    me

342 *sty me*: pen me up like a pig.

In this hard rock, whiles you do keep from me
The rest o'th' island.

Prospero
                   Thou most lying slave,

345 *stripes*: beatings.

345 Whom stripes may move, not kindness, I have us'd
    thee—

346 *humane*: The stress is on the first
syllable; this is the spelling of the Folio
text—although at the time there was
little distinction between 'human' and
'humane'.

Filth as thou art—with humane care, and lodg'd
    thee
In mine own cell, till thou didst seek to violate
The honour of my child.

Caliban
              O ho, O ho! Would't had been done!
Thou didst prevent me—I had peopled else

350–61 The hatred and revulsion expressed
in this speech shows an unexpected side
to the hitherto placid and docile
Miranda—and many editors of the
eighteenth and nineteenth centuries
re-assigned the words to Prospero.
351 *print*: imprint, impression.
352 *capable of*: susceptible [only] to.

350 This isle with Calibans.

Miranda
                Abhorred slave,
Which any print of goodness wilt not take,
Being capable of all ill! I pitied thee,
Took pains to make thee speak, taught thee each
    hour
One thing or other. When thou didst not, savage,
355 Know thine own meaning, but wouldst gabble like
A thing most brutish, I endow'd thy purposes

357 *race*: disposition.

With words that made them known. But thy vile
    race—
Though thou didst learn—had that in't which good
    natures
Could not abide to be with; therefore wast thou
360 Deservedly confin'd into this rock,
Who hadst deserv'd more than a prison.

Caliban
You taught me language, and my profit on't

363 *red*: bleeding, spotted.
   rid: destroy.

Is I know how to curse. The red plague rid you
For learning me your language!

Prospero

                                        Hag-seed, hence!
365 Fetch us in fuel, and be quick, thou'rt best,
     To answer other business—shrug'st thou, malice?
     If thou neglect'st, or dost unwillingly
     What I command, I'll rack thee with old cramps,
     Fill all thy bones with aches, make thee roar,
370 That beats shall tremble at thy din.

Caliban

                                        No, pray thee.
     [*Aside*] I must obey. His art is of such power,
     It would control my dam's god Setebos
     And make a vassal of him.

Prospero

                                        So, slave, hence!
                                        [*Exit* Caliban

          Enter Ferdinand, *and* Ariel *invisible,*
                    playing and singing

     Ariel [*Sings*]
     Come unto these yellow sands,
375   And then take hands;
     Curtsied when you have, and kiss'd
          The wild waves whist,
     Foot it featly here and there,
          And sweet sprites bear
380 The burden. Hark, hark!
               [*Burden, dispersedly*] Bow-wow.
          The watch dogs bark.
               [*Burden, dispersedly*] Bow-wow.
          Hark, hark! I hear
385 The strain of strutting Chanticleer
          Cry cock a diddle dow.
               [*Burden, dispersedly*] Cock a diddle dow.

     Ferdinand
     Where should this music be?—i'th' air or th' earth?
     It sounds no more; and sure it waits upon
390 Some god o'th' island. Sitting on a bank,
     Weeping again the king my father's wreck,
     This music crept by me upon the waters,
     Allaying both their fury and my passion
     With its sweet air. Thence I have follow'd it,

366 *answer other business*: get on with your other jobs.

368 *old cramps*: the cramps of old age.

369 *aches*: The word was pronounced with two syllables.

372 *Setebos*: The name is found in accounts of Magellan's voyages as that of 'a great devil' of the Patagonians.

373s.d. *invisible*: Since Ariel was told (line 301) to appear as a sea-nymph, it must be assumed here that he is invisible only to Ferdinand.
     playing: Ariel's instrument is most probably the lute.

376–7 *kissed . . . whist*: kissed the wild waves into silence.

378 *featly*: daintily, elegantly.

380 *burden*: refrain.

381s.d. *dispersedly*: i.e. not in unison.

385 *strain*: song.
     Chanticleer: the traditional name for a cock.

389 *waits*: attends.

393 *passion*: suffering.

394 *air*: tune, sound.

395 Or it hath drawn me rather; but 'tis gone.
No, it begins again.

    Ariel [*Sings*]
    Full fathom five thy father lies,
    Of his bones are coral made;
    Those are pearls that were his eyes;
400   Nothing of him that doth fade,
    But doth suffer a sea-change
    Into something rich and strange.
    Sea nymphs hourly ring his knell.
      [*Burden*] Ding dong.
405 Hark, now I hear them, ding dong bell.

    Ferdinand
The ditty does remember my drown'd father.
This is no mortal business, nor no sound
That the earth owes—I hear it now above me.

    Prospero
[*To* Miranda]
The fringed curtains of thine eye advance,
410 And say what thou seest yond.

    Miranda
                       What is't?—a spirit?
Lord, how it looks about! Believe me, sir,
It carries a brave form. But 'tis a spirit.

    Prospero
No, wench, it eats and sleeps, and hath such senses
As we have—such. This gallant which thou seest
415 Was in the wreck, and but he's something stain'd
With grief—that's beauty's canker—thou mightst
    call him
A goodly person. He hath lost his fellows,
And strays about to find 'em.

    Miranda
                     I might call him
A thing divine, for nothing natural
420 I ever saw so noble.

    Prospero
[*Aside*]   It goes on, I see,
As my soul prompts it. [*To* Ariel] Spirit, fine spirit,
    I'll free thee
Within two days for this.

---

397 *Full fathom five*: all of five fathoms (= 30 feet deep). The original music for song of Ariel is printed on p. 100.

398 *are*: The nearby plural noun 'bones' attracts the plural form of the verb.

406 *ditty*: lyric, song.
    remember: commemorate.
407 *mortal*: human.
408 *owes*: owns.

412 *brave*: fine, handsome.

414 *gallant*: fine gentleman.
415 *but*: except for the fact that.
    something: somewhat.
416 *canker*: destroyer—the disease or rust that corrodes from the inside.

419 *natural*: Miranda's experience is very limited—see line 480.

420 *It goes on*: my plan is working.

422 *Most sure, the goddess*: Ferdinand
responds to the sight of Miranda with
the words of Virgil's hero Aeneas: *O dea
certe* (*Aeneid*, i, 328). See 'Source',
p. xxx.
423 *these airs*: this music—i.e. Ariel's songs.
424 *May know*: that I may know.
remain: reside.
426 *bear me*: conduct myself.
428 *If you . . . or no*: whether or not you are
married.

430 *the best*: Ferdinand, believing his father
to be drowned, assumes that he has
succeeded to the throne of Naples.
431 *How?*: what do you mean?
432 *wert thou*: would you be.

433 *A single thing*: one and the same thing.
434 *Naples*: the King of Naples.
435 *that*: because.
436 *never . . . ebb*: which have never been
dry since then.

439 *his brave son*: Nowhere else in the play is
there mention of a son for Antonio—
perhaps Shakespeare forgot, or changed
his mind, about this.
440 *control thee*: challenge you about that.

442 *chang'd*: interchanged.
Delicate: exquisite.

444 *I fear . . . wrong*: i.e. in claiming to be
King of Naples.

447 *sigh'd for*: was attracted to.

Ferdinand

                   Most sure, the goddess
On whom these airs attend. Vouchsafe my prayer
May know if you remain upon this island,
425 And that you will some good instruction give
How I may bear me here. My prime request,
Which I do last pronounce, is—O you wonder!—
If you be maid or no?
  Miranda
                      No wonder, sir,
But certainly a maid.
    Ferdinand
                   My language! Heavens!
430 I am the best of them that speak this speech,
Were I but where 'tis spoken.
  Prospero
                    How? The best?
What wert thou if the King of Naples heard thee?
    Ferdinand
A single thing, as I am now, that wonders
To hear thee speak of Naples. He does hear me,
435 And that he does, I weep: myself am Naples,
Who with mine eyes, never since at ebb, beheld
The king my father wreck'd.
  Miranda
                 Alack, for mercy!
    Ferdinand
Yes, faith, and all his lords, the Duke of Milan
And his brave son being twain.
  Prospero
[*Aside*]   The Duke of Milan
440 And his more braver daughter could control thee
If now 'twere fit to do't. At the first sight
They have chang'd eyes. Delicate Ariel,
I'll set thee free for this.—A word, good sir:
I fear you have done yourself some wrong; a word.
  Miranda
445 Why speaks my father so ungently? This
Is the third man that e'er I saw, the first
That e'er I sigh'd for. Pity move my father
To be inclin'd my way!

449 *gone forth*: elsewhere engaged.

450 *Soft*: just a minute.

452 *uneasy*: difficult.
452–3 *too light . . . prize light*: winning the
  prize too easily might cheapen it.

458–60 Miranda expresses a conventional
  notion of Renaissance Neoplatonic
  philosophy, that beauty of spirit and
  beauty of form are inseparable.

464 *fresh-brook mussels*: Fresh-water mussels
  are inedible.

466 *entertainment*: treatment.

469 *gentle . . . fearful*: of noble birth and
  [therefore] not a coward.

470 *My foot my tutor*: shall I be told what to
  do by something that is beneath me.

Ferdinand
                                O, if a virgin,
And your affection not gone forth, I'll make you
450 The Queen of Naples.
  Prospero
                        Soft, sir, one word more.
[*Aside*] They are both in either's powers; but this
  swift business
I must uneasy make lest too light winning
Make the prize light.—One word more: I charge
  thee
That thou attend me. Thou dost here usurp
455 The name thou ow'st not, and hast put thyself
Upon this island as a spy, to win it
From me, the lord on't.
  Ferdinand
                        No, as I am a man!
  Miranda
There's nothing ill can dwell in such a temple.
If the ill spirit have so fair a house,
460 Good things will strive to dwell with't.
  Prospero
                                Follow me.—
Speak not you for him: he's a traitor.—Come,
I'll manacle thy neck and feet together.
Sea-water shalt thou drink; thy food shall be
The fresh-brook mussels, withered roots, and husks
465 Wherein the acorn cradled. Follow.
  Ferdinand
                                No;
I will resist such entertainment till
Mine enemy has more power.

          He draws, and is charmed from moving

  Miranda
                        O dear father,
Make not too rash a trial of him, for
He's gentle, and not fearful.
  Prospero
                        What, I say—
470 My foot my tutor? Put thy sword up, traitor,
Who mak'st a show but dar'st not strike, thy
  conscience

472 *ward*: defensive posture.
473 *stick*: i.e. his magician's wand.

Is so possess'd with guilt. Come from thy ward,
For I can here disarm thee with this stick
And make thy weapon drop.

Miranda
                              Beseech you, father—
Prospero
475 Hence! Hang not on my garments.
Miranda
                                        Sir, have pity;
I'll be his surety.
Prospero
                    Silence! One word more
Shall make me chide thee, if not hate thee. What,
An advocate for an impostor? Hush!
Thou think'st there is no more such shapes as he,
480 Having seen but him and Caliban. Foolish wench,

481 *To*: compared to.

To th' most of men this is a Caliban,
And they to him are angels.
Miranda
                            My affections
Are then most humble. I have no ambition
To see a goodlier man.
Prospero
[*To* Ferdinand]   Come on, obey.

485 *nerves . . . infancy*: sinews are like a
baby's.

485 Thy nerves are in their infancy again
And have no vigour in them.
Ferdinand
                            So they are.
My spirits, as in a dream, are all bound up.

488–90 *My father's loss . . . me*: Ferdinand's
bewilderment speaks through the
confused syntax: the loss of his father,
and all other griefs, would be nothing to
him.
489 *nor*: not even.
492–3 *All . . . use of*: let those who are free
enjoy every other part of the world.

My father's loss, the weakness which I feel,
The wreck of all my friends, nor this man's threats,
490 To whom I am subdued, are but light to me,
Might I but through my prison once a day
Behold this maid. All corners else o' th' earth
Let liberty make use of—space enough
Have I in such a prison.
Prospero
[*Aside*]   It works. [*To* Ferdinand] Come on.—
495 [*To* Ariel] Thou hast done well, fine Ariel. Follow
    me;

496 *do me*: do for me.

Hark what thou else shalt do me.

Miranda

[*To* Ferdinand]   Be of comfort.
My father's of a better nature, sir,
Than he appears by speech. This is unwonted
Which now came from him.

Prospero

[*To* Ariel]   Thou shalt be as free
500 As mountain winds; but then exactly do
All points of my command.

Ariel

                              To th' syllable.

Prospero

[*To* Ferdinand] Come, follow. [*To* Miranda]—Speak
not for him.

                              [*Exeunt*

498 *unwonted*: uncharacteristic.

Act 2

Act 2   Scene 1

In a different part of the island (see
1, 2, 220), members of the king's party reveal
their different temperaments in their
reactions to the shipwreck: Gonzalo looks on
the bright side of things; Alonso is
despairing; Sebastian and Antonio are
flippant. Whilst the two older men are
sleeping, Sebastian urges Antonio to murder
the king, but Ariel arrives in time to foil their
plot.

3 *much beyond*: of far greater importance.
   hint of: occasion for.

5 *masters . . . merchant*: owners of some
   merchant-ship, and the ship itself.

11 *porridge*: Sebastian makes a pun with
   'peace' (line 9) and 'pease-porridge'.

12 *visitor*: Gonzalo is likened to the church
   functionary who was delegated to visit
   the sick.
   give him o'er so: leave him alone so
   easily.

14 *strike*: Striking and chiming watches
   were fashionable at this time.

16 *One. Tell*: Sebastian pretends that the
   'watch' has just struck one, and he
   wants Antonio to keep count.

17–18 *when . . . entertainer*: when a man
   gets distressed over everything that
   happens, then—.

19 *dollar*: i.e. in payment; Sebastian
   quibbles on *entertainer* = performer, and
   in the next line Gonzalo counters his
   quibble.

Scene 1

Enter Alonso, Sebastian, Antonio,
Gonzalo, Adrian, Francisco

Gonzalo
[*To* Alonso] Beseech you, sir, be merry. You have
  cause—
So have we all—of joy, for our escape
Is much beyond our loss. Our hint of woe
Is common: every day some sailor's wife,
5 The masters of some merchant, and the merchant
Have just our theme of woe; but for the miracle—
I mean our preservation—few in millions
Can speak like us. Then wisely, good sir, weigh
Our sorrow with our comfort.
    Alonso
                      Prithee, peace.
    Sebastian
10 [*Aside to* Antonio] He receives comfort like cold
porridge.
    Antonio
The visitor will not give him o'er so.
    Sebastian
Look, he's winding up the watch of his wit. By and
by it will strike.
    Gonzalo
15 Sir,—
    Sebastian
One. Tell.
    Gonzalo
—when every grief is entertain'd
That's offer'd, comes to th' entertainer—
    Sebastian
A dollar.

Gonzalo

20 Dolour comes to him indeed. You have spoken truer
than you purposed.

Sebastian

You have taken it wiselier than I meant you should.

Gonzalo

Therefore, my lord,—

Antonio

Fie, what a spendthrift is he of his tongue!

Alonso

25 [*To* Gonzalo] I prithee, spare.

Gonzalo

Well, I have done. But yet—

Sebastian

He will be talking.

Antonio

Which, of he or Adrian, for a good wager, first
begins to crow?

Sebastian

30 The old cock.

Antonio

The cockerel.

Sebastian

Done. The wager?

Antonio

A laughter.

Sebastian

A match!

Adrian

35 Though this island seem to be desert—

Antonio

Ha, ha, ha!

Sebastian

So, you're paid!

Adrian

Uninhabitable, and almost inaccessible—

Sebastian

Yet—

Adrian

40 Yet—

Antonio

He could not miss't.

30 *The old cock*: i.e. Gonzalo; the proverb was 'The young cock crows as he the old one hears'.

35 *desert*: uninhabitable.

37 *So . . . paid*: there you are, you've had your laugh.

42 *subtle*: gentle.

43 *temperance*: climate.

44 *delicate wench*: Antonio perversely mistakes Adrian's meaning.

45 *subtle*: crafty, sexually clever.

Adrian
It must needs be of subtle, tender, and delicate temperance.

Antonio
Temperance was a delicate wench.

Sebastian
45 Ay, and a subtle, as he most learnedly delivered.

Adrian
The air breathes upon us here most sweetly.

Sebastian
As if it had lungs, and rotten ones.

Antonio
Or as 'twere perfumed by a fen.

Gonzalo
Here is everything advantageous to life.

Antonio
50 True, save means to live.

Sebastian
Of that there's none or little.

Gonzalo
How lush and lusty the grass looks! How green!

52 *lush*: tender.

53 *tawny*: reddish-brown; either Antonio, with his usual perversity, contradicts Gonzalo—or perhaps appearances on the island vary according to the eye of the beholder.

54 *eye*: touch.

Antonio
The ground indeed is tawny.

Sebastian
With an eye of green in't.

Antonio
55 He misses not much.

Sebastian
No, he doth but mistake the truth totally.

Gonzalo
But the rarity of it is, which is indeed almost beyond credit—

Sebastian
As many vouched rarities are.

59 *vouched rarities*: things said to be 'rarities'.

60–3 *our garments . . . water*: Ariel told Prospero that this was the case (*1, 2,* 218–19).

Gonzalo
60 That our garments, being, as they were, drenched in the sea, hold notwithstanding their freshness and gloss, being rather new-dyed than stained with salt water.

Antonio
If but one of his pockets could speak, would it not 65 say he lies?

66 *pocket up*: hide, or suppress.

67–9 *we . . . Tunis*: Gonzalo supplies the
audience with necessary information—
and provides a fresh topic of debate for
the courtiers.

74–7 *widow Dido . . . 'widower Aeneas'*:
Dido, the Queen of Carthage whose
love for Aeneas is the subject of
Book IV of the *Aeneid*, was the widow
of Sychaeus; Aeneas's wife, Creusa, was
killed at the sack of Troy. See 'Source',
p. xxx.

79 *study of*: think about.

81 *This . . . was Carthage*: Tunis now is
what Carthage used to be: following the
destruction of Carthage, Tunis took its
place as political and commercial centre
of the region.

84 *miraculous harp*: The music of
Amphion's harp was able to raise the
walls of Thebes—but Gonzalo's word
has rebuilt the entire city of Carthage.

89 *kernels*: pips.

91 *Ay*: The reason for Gonzalo's utterance
is not very clear.

Sebastian
Ay, or very falsely pocket up his report.
   Gonzalo
Methinks our garments are now as fresh as when we
put them on first in Afric, at the marriage of the
king's fair daughter Claribel to the King of Tunis.
   Sebastian
70 'Twas a sweet marriage, and we prosper well in our
return.
   Adrian
Tunis was never graced before with such a paragon
to their queen.
   Gonzalo
Not since widow Dido's time.
   Antonio
75 Widow? A pox o' that. How came that widow in?
Widow Dido!
   Sebastian
What if he had said 'widower Aeneas' too? Good
lord, how you take it!
   Adrian
'Widow Dido' said you? You make me study of that.
80 She was of Carthage, not of Tunis.
   Gonzalo
This Tunis, sir, was Carthage.
   Adrian
Carthage?
   Gonzalo
I assure you, Carthage.
   Antonio
His word is more than the miraculous harp.
   Sebastian
85 He hath raised the wall, and houses too.
   Antonio
What impossible matter will he make easy next?
   Sebastian
I think he will carry this island home in his pocket
and give it his son for an apple.
   Antonio
And sowing the kernels of it in the sea, bring forth
90 more islands.
   Gonzalo
Ay.

92 *in good time*: about time too.
97 *Bate*: but don't mention.

100 *in a sort*: in a way.
101 *fished for*: Antonio takes Gonzalo's 'sort' with the metaphor of drawing lots.
103 *cram*: The image is of force-feeding.

104 *stomach of my sense*: appetite for such comfort *and also* understanding of the situation.
106 *rate*: estimation.

117–18 *that . . . relieve him*: Gonzalo describes an overhanging cliff, its base eroded by the sea, which seemed to bend over in compassion.

Antonio
Why, in good time.
   Gonzalo
[*To* Alonso] Sir, we were talking that our garments
   seem now as fresh as when we were at Tunis at the
95 marriage of your daughter, who is now queen.
   Antonio
And the rarest that e'er came there.
   Sebastian
Bate, I beseech you, widow Dido.
   Antonio
O, widow Dido? Ay, widow Dido.
   Gonzalo
Is not, sir, my doublet as fresh as the first day I wore
100 it? I mean, in a sort.
   Antonio
That sort was well fished for.
   Gonzalo
When I wore it at your daughter's marriage.
   Alonso
You cram these words into mine ears against
   The stomach of my sense. Would I had never
105 Married my daughter there, for coming thence
   My son is lost, and, in my rate, she too,
   Who is so far from Italy remov'd
   I ne'er again shall see her. O thou mine heir
   Of Naples and of Milan, what strange fish
110 Hath made his meal on thee?
   Francisco
                                    Sir, he may live.
   I saw him beat the surges under him
   And ride upon their backs; he trod the water,
   Whose enmity he flung aside, and breasted
   The surge most swoll'n that met him; his bold head
115 'Bove the contentious waves he kept, and oar'd
   Himself with his good arms in lusty stroke
   To th' shore, that o'er his wave-worn basis bow'd,
   As stooping to relieve him. I not doubt
   He came alive to land.
   Alonso
                                    No, no, he's gone.

Sebastian

120 Sir, you may thank yourself for this great loss,
That would not bless our Europe with your
            daughter,
But rather lose her to an African,
Where she, at least, is banish'd from your eye,
Who hath cause to wet the grief on't.

Alonso

                                    Prithee, peace.

Sebastian

125 You were kneel'd to and importun'd otherwise
By all of us, and the fair soul herself
Weigh'd between loathness and obedience at
Which end o'th' beam should bow. We have lost
            your son,
I fear, for ever. Milan and Naples have
130 More widows in them of this business' making
Than we bring men to comfort them.
The fault's your own.

Alonso

                        So is the dear'st o'th' loss

Gonzalo

My lord Sebastian,
The truth you speak doth lack some gentleness,
135 And time to speak it in—you rub the sore
When you should bring the plaster.

Sebastian

                                    Very well.

Antonio

And most chirurgeonly!

Gonzalo

[*To* Alonso] It is foul weather in us all, good sir,
When you are cloudy.

Sebastian

                        Foul weather?

Antonio

                                    Very foul.

Gonzalo

140 [*To* Alonso] Had I plantation of this isle, my lord,—

Antonio

He'd sow't with nettle-seed.

Sebastian

                        Or docks, or mallows.

124 *wet . . . on't*: weep over the sorrow of it.

125 *importun'd*: The stress is on the second syllable.
127–8 *Weigh'd . . . bow*: Alonso's daughter had to decide which weighed the heavier for her, dislike of the proposed marriage or obedience to her father.

131 *Than we bring men*: Sebastian assumes that the king's party will return to Naples, but that the rest of the fleet has been lost.

135 *time*: the appropriate time.

137 *chirurgeonly*: like a surgeon.

138–9 *foul . . . Foul . . . foul*: Sebastian and Antonio take the opportunity for a pun with 'fowl' and 'fool'.

140 *plantation*: the right to colonize, *and*, the freedom to plant.
141 *docks*: dock-leaves, inimical to cultivation but a popular antidote to nettle-stings.
   mallows: weeds used to make soothing ointment for nettle-stings.

Gonzalo

—And were the king on't, what would I do?

Sebastian

'Scape being drunk, for want of wine.

Gonzalo

I'th' commonwealth I would by contraries

145 Execute all things, for no kind of traffic

Would I admit; no name of magistrate;

Letters should not be known; riches, poverty,

And use of service, none; contract, succession,

Bourn, bound of land, tilth, vineyard, none;

150 No use of metal, corn, or wine, or oil;

No occupation, all men idle, all,

And women too, but innocent and pure;

No sovereignty—

Sebastian

　　　　　　　Yet he would be king on't.

Antonio

The latter end of his commonwealth forgets the

155 beginning.

Gonzalo

All things in common nature should produce

Without sweat or endeavour. Treason, felony,

Sword, pike, knife, gun, or need of any engine

Would I not have, but nature should bring forth

160 Of it own kind all foison, all abundance

To feed my innocent people.

Sebastian

No marrying 'mong his subjects?

Antonio

None, man, all idle—whores and knaves.

Gonzalo

I would with such perfection govern, sir,

165 T'excel the golden age.

Sebastian

'Save his majesty!

Antonio

Long live Gonzalo!

Gonzalo

And—do you mark me, sir?

Alonso

Prithee no more. Thou dost talk nothing to me.

144–65 *I'th' commonwealth . . . age*: Gonzalo's political philosophy is based on a section of Montaigne's essay 'Of the Cannibals' (see 'Shakespeare's Sources', p. 91).

144 *by contraries*: quite otherwise (i.e. from the usual manner).

145 *traffic*: commerce.

147 *Letters*: literature, academic education.

148 *use of service*: keeping servants.
contract: bargaining, property dealing.
succession: inheritance.

149 *Bourn, bound*: boundary, limit (the words are synonymous).
tilth: arable land.

152 *innocent and pure*: Gonzalo forestalls the proverb, 'Idleness begets lust'.

156 *in common*: for general use.

158 *engine*: instrument of war.

160 *it*: its.
foison: harvest.

163 *None*: Antonio would presumably argue that marriage is also a contract (line 148), and therefore irrelevant among the 'innocent people'.

165 *golden age*: the imagined period in a people's history when everything was perfect.

166 *'Save*: God save.

Gonzalo

170 I do well believe your highness, and did it to minister
occasion to these gentlemen, who are of such
sensible and nimble lungs that they always use to
laugh at nothing.

Antonio

'Twas you we laughed at.

Gonzalo

175 Who in this kind of merry fooling am nothing to
you; so you may continue, and laugh at nothing still.

Antonio

What a blow was there given!

Sebastian

An it had not fall'n flat-long.

Gonzalo

You are gentlemen of brave mettle; you would lift the
180 moon out of her sphere if she would continue in it
five weeks without changing.

Enter Ariel *invisible, playing solemn music*

Sebastian

We would so, and then go a-bat-fowling.

Antonio

Nay, good my lord, be not angry.

170–1 *minister occasion*: provide an
opportunity.

172 *sensible*: sensitive.
use: are accustomed.

178 *An*: if.
flat-long: on the flat side of the sword,
harmlessly.
179 *mettle*: spirit; Gonzalo puns on the
'sword' metaphor.
179–81 *you would . . . changing*: you would
try to steal the moon out of the sky if it
did not change every month.

182 *a-bat-fowling*: stealing birds at roost in
the darkness.

184–5 *adventure . . . weakly*: risk my good
judgement by being so silly (as to be
angry with them).

Gonzalo
No, I warrant you, I will not adventure my discretion
185 so weakly. Will you laugh me asleep, for I am very
heavy?

186 *heavy*: drowsy.

Antonio
Go sleep, and hear us.

187 *Go . . . hear us*: settle yourselves down
to sleep, and you can listen to us.

All sleep except Alonso, Sebastian, *and*
Antonio

Alonso
What, all so soon asleep? I wish mine eyes
Would, with themselves, shut up my thoughts. I find
190 They are inclin'd to do so.

Sebastian
                                    Please you, sir,
Do not omit the heavy offer of it.
It seldom visits sorrow; when it doth,
It is a comforter.

191 *omit*: disregard.
heavy offer: serious opportunity.

Antonio
                          We two, my lord,
Will guard your person while you take your rest,
195 And watch your safety.

195 *watch*: protect.

Alonso
                                Thank you. Wondrous heavy.

Alonso *sleeps*   [*Exit* Ariel

Sebastian
What a strange drowsiness possesses them!
Antonio
It is the quality o'th' climate.
Sebastian
                                          Why
Doth it not then our eyelids sink? I find not
Myself dispos'd to sleep.
Antonio
                                    Nor I; my spirits are nimble.

199 *nimble*: lively.
200 *consent*: common agreement.

200 They fell together all, as by consent;
They dropp'd as by a thunder-stroke. What might,
Worthy Sebastian, O what might—? No more.
And yet methinks I see it in thy face,
What thou shouldst be. Th' occasion speaks thee,
and

204 *Th' occasion speaks thee*: the opportunity
calls to you.

205 My strong imagination sees a crown
Dropping upon thy head.

Sebastian
                                    What? Art thou waking?

Antonio
Do you not hear me speak?

Sebastian
                                    I do, and surely
It is a sleepy language, and thou speak'st
Out of thy sleep. What is it thou didst say?
210 This is a strange repose, to be asleep
With eyes wide open—standing, speaking, moving,
And yet so fast asleep.

Antonio
                                    Noble Sebastian,
Thou let'st thy fortune sleep—die, rather; wink'st
Whiles thou art waking.

Sebastian
                                    Thou dost snore distinctly.
215 There's meaning in thy snores.

Antonio
I am more serious than my custom. You
Must be so too, if heed me; which to do
Trebles thee o'er.

Sebastian
                                    Well? I am standing water.

Antonio
I'll teach you how to flow.

Sebastian
                                    Do so—to ebb
220 Hereditary sloth instructs me.

Antonio
                                    O!
If you but knew how you the purpose cherish
Whiles thus you mock it, how in stripping it
You more invest it—ebbing men, indeed,
Most often do so near the bottom run
225 By their own fear or sloth.

Sebastian
                                    Prithee say on.
The setting of thine eye and cheek proclaim
A matter from thee, and a birth, indeed,
Which throes thee much to yield.

---

206 *waking*: awake.

213 *wink'st*: close your eyes.

214 *distinctly*: articulately, understandably.

217 *if heed me*: if you listen to me.
218 *Trebles thee o'er*: makes you three times as great.
218 *I am standing water*: I am waiting to be moved.

219–20 *to ebb . . . me*: the lethargy which I was born with teaches me how to withdraw; Sebastian perhaps implies that his position as younger brother to Alonso has also enforced lethargy.
221–2 *If you . . . mock it*: you make the situation worse all the time that you are scoffing at it.
222–3 *in stripping . . . invest it*: the more you put it off, the greater the importance that you give to it.

226 *setting*: fixed expression.
227 *A matter*: something important.
228 *throes thee*: gives you much labour-pain.

229 *lord of weak remembrance*: i.e. Gonzalo,
    whose memory is weak (perhaps
    because in his description of the ideal
    commonwealth of which he would be
    king, he would have no ruler—see
    line 153).
231 *earth'd*: dead and buried.
232 *spirit of persuasion*: a persuader.
232–3 *only . . . persuade*: giving counsel is his
    only occupation.

237–40 *No hope . . . there*: because you have
    no hope of Ferdinand's safety, you can
    have much greater hope of achieving
    the throne of Naples legitimately than
    even the most ambitious man could
    look for without fear of being
    discovered. Antonio is unsure how
    Sebastian will receive his promptings,
    and his lines stumble in their syntax.
239 *pierce a wink*: catch a glimpse.
240 *grant*: agree.

244 *Ten . . . life*: further than a man can
    travel in a lifetime. Antonio grossly
    exaggerates the distance: Tunis is about
    300 miles from Naples—and in fact the
    king's party has just been visiting there
    for the wedding of Claribel.
245 *note*: information.
    post: messenger.
246 *man . . . slow*: Whereas the sun rises
    every day, the moon takes a month to
    go round the earth.
247 *from*: coming from.
248 *cast*: cast ashore—but the initial
    meaning gives way to a theatrical usage.
249 *by that destiny*: by the same destiny that
    cast us ashore we were singled out to
    perform this action.
251 *yours . . . discharge*: for you and me to
    perform.

Antonio
                                Thus, sir:
Although this lord of weak remembrance, this,
230 Who shall be of as little memory
When he is earth'd, hath here almost persuaded—
For he's a spirit of persuasion, only
Professes to persuade—the king his son's alive,
'Tis as impossible that he's undrown'd
235 As he that sleeps here swims.
    Sebastian
                                I have no hope
That he's undrown'd.
    Antonio
                                O, out of that no hope
What great hope have you! No hope that way is
Another way so high a hope that even
Ambition cannot pierce a wink beyond,
240 But doubt discovery there. Will you grant with me
That Ferdinand is drown'd?
    Sebastian
                                He's gone.
    Antonio
                                Then tell me,
Who's the next heir of Naples?
    Sebastian
                                Claribel.
    Antonio
She that is queen of Tunis; she that dwells
Ten leagues beyond man's life; she that from Naples
245 Can have no note unless the sun were post—
The man i'th' moon's too slow—till newborn chins
Be rough and razorable; she that from whom
We all were sea-swallow'd, though some cast again—
And by that destiny, to perform an act
250 Whereof what's past is prologue, what to come
In yours and my discharge.
    Sebastian
                                What stuff is this? How say you?
'Tis true my brother's daughter's queen of Tunis,
So is she heir of Naples, 'twixt which regions
There is some space.

254 *cubit*: a measure that varied from time
    to time and place to place, usually
    about 18 inches (45 centimetres), the
    length of the forearm.
256 *Measure us*: travel, traverse.
    Keep: stay.
257 *wake*: wake himself up.
259 *There be*: there are those.

262–3 *I myself . . . chat*: I could teach a
    jackdaw to speak as profoundly as he
    does.

266–7 *content . . . fortune*: are you inclined to
    look favourably on your lucky chance.

270 *feater*: more suitably.

273 *kibe*: chilblain.

276 *candied*: frozen, congealed.
277 *molest*: interfere with me, get in my way.

281 *thus*: Antonio mimes the gesture of
    stabbing Gonzalo.
283 *morsel*: bit of flesh.
284 *upbraid*: rebuke.
285 *suggestion*: incitement to evil.

Antonio

         A space whose every cubit
255 Seems to cry out, 'How shall that Claribel
 Measure us back to Naples? Keep in Tunis,
 And let Sebastian wake.' Say this were death
 That now hath seiz'd them, why, they were no worse
 Than now they are. There be that can rule Naples
260 As well as he that sleeps, lords that can prate
 As amply and unnecessarily
 As this Gonzalo; I myself could make
 A chough of as deep chat. O, that you bore
 The mind that I do, what a sleep were this
265 For your advancement! Do you understand me?

Sebastian

Methinks I do.

Antonio

        And how does your content
 Tender your own good fortune?

Sebastian

            I remember
 You did supplant your brother Prospero.

Antonio

              True;
 And look how well my garments sit upon me,
270 Much feater than before. My brother's servants
 Were then my fellows, now they are my men.

Sebastian

But for your conscience?

Antonio

Ay, sir, where lies that? If 'twere a kibe
 'Twould put me to my slipper, but I feel not
275 This deity in my bosom. Twenty consciences
 That stand 'twixt me and Milan, candied be they,
 And melt ere they molest! Here lies your brother,
 No better than the earth he lies upon,
 If he were that which now he's like—that's dead—
280 Whom I with this obedient steel, three inches of it,
 Can lay to bed for ever; whiles you, doing thus,
 To the perpetual wink for aye might put
 This ancient morsel, this Sir Prudence, who
 Should not upbraid our course. For all the rest,
285 They'll take suggestion as a cat laps milk;

286–7 *tell . . . hour*: i.e. agree to anything that we propose.

287 *case*: situation.

290 *the tribute*: i.e. the tribute referred to by Prospero (*1*, *2*, 123–4).

293 *fall it*: let it fall.
293s.d. *apart*: aside from the audience.
invisible: i.e. to the other characters.
with music and song: Ariel is perhaps accompanied by other spirits forming a musical consort.

303 *be sudden*: act quickly.

305 *you*: i.e. your swords.
306 *Wherefore . . . looking*: why do you look so frightened.

They'll tell the clock to any business that
We say befits the hour.

Sebastian   Thy case, dear friend,
Shall be my precedent: as thou got'st Milan,
I'll come by Naples. Draw thy sword—one stroke
290 Shall free thee from the tribute which thou payest,
And I the king shall love thee.

Antonio   Draw together,
And when I rear my hand do you the like
To fall it on Gonzalo.

Sebastian
                                    O, but one word.

They talk apart

Enter Ariel, *invisible, with music and song*

Ariel
My master through his art foresees the danger
295 That you, his friend, are in, and sends me forth—
For else his project dies—to keep them living.

He sings in Gonzalo's *ear*

While you here do snoring lie,
Open-eyed conspiracy
    His time doth take.
300 If of life you keep a care,
Shake off slumber, and beware.
    Awake, awake!

Antonio
Then let us both be sudden.

Gonzalo
[*Waking*]   Now, good angels
Preserve the king!

The others wake

Alonso
305 Why, how now, ho! Awake? Why are you drawn?
Wherefore this ghastly looking?

Gonzalo
                                    What's the matter?

307 *securing*: protecting.

Sebastian
Whiles we stood here securing your repose,
Even now, we heard a hollow burst of bellowing,
Like bulls, or rather lions—did't not wake you?
310 It struck mine ear most terribly.
    Alonso
                                        I heard nothing.
    Antonio
O, 'twas a din to fright a monster's ear,
To make an earthquake. Sure, it was the roar
Of a whole herd of lions.
    Alonso
                                Heard you this, Gonzalo?
    Gonzalo
Upon mine honour sir, I heard a humming,
315 And that a strange one too, which did awake me.
I shak'd you, sir, and cried. As mine eyes open'd
I saw their weapons drawn. There was a noise,

318 *verily*: true.

That's verily. 'Tis best we stand upon our guard,
Or that we quit this place. Let's draw our weapons.
    Alonso
320 Lead off this ground, and let's make further search
For my poor son.
    Gonzalo
                        Heavens keep him from these beasts!
For he is sure i' th' island.
    Alonso
                                Lead away.
    Ariel
Prospero my lord shall know what I have done.
So, king, go safely on to seek thy son.
                                            [*Exeunt*

324 *Exeunt*: Ariel and the king's party
    probably depart in different directions.

Act 2   Scene 2

Caliban curses Prospero. Trinculo discovers
Caliban and takes refuge from the storm.
Stephano, with his bottle, discovers Trinculo.
Caliban discovers wine, and worships a new
god.

2 *flats*: swamps.
3 *By inchmeal*: inch by inch all over.

4 *needs must*: am forced to.
  nor: neither.
5 *urchin-shows*: goblin apparitions in the
  form of hedgehogs ('urchins').
6 *firebrand*: flaming torch.

9 *mow*: grimace, make mouths.

13 *wound with*: entwined by.

17 *mind*: notice.
18 *bear off*: keep off.
20 *Yon*: yonder.
21 *bombard*: an early form of cannon,
   which gave its name to a large jug or
   bottle; Trinculo has both senses in
   mind.

26 *poor-John*: dried, salted fish.
28 *painted*: i.e. on a sign, to attract
   spectators.

Scene 2

Enter Caliban *with a burden of wood*

Caliban
All the infections that the sun sucks up
From bogs, fens, flats, on Prosper fall, and make him
By inchmeal a disease!

A noise of thunder heard

His spirits hear me,
And yet I needs must curse. But they'll nor pinch
5 Fright me with urchin-shows, pitch me i'th' mire,
Nor lead me like a firebrand in the dark
Out of my way, unless he bid 'em; but
For every trifle are they set upon me,
Sometime like apes that mow and chatter at me,
10 And after bite me; then like hedgehogs, which
Lie tumbling in my barefoot way, and mount
Their pricks at my footfall; sometime am I
All wound with adders, who with cloven tongues
Do hiss me into madness—

Enter Trinculo

Lo, now, lo,
15 Here comes a spirit of his, and to torment me
For bringing wood in slowly. I'll fall flat.
Perchance he will not mind me.

He lies down and covers himself with his cloak

Trinculo
Here's neither bush nor shrub to bear off any weather
at all, and another storm brewing—I hear it sing i'th'
20 wind. Yon same black cloud, yon huge one, looks like
a foul bombard that would shed his liquor. If it should
thunder as it did before, I know not where to hide my
head—yon same cloud cannot choose but fall by
pailfuls. What have we here—a man or a fish?—dead
25 or alive? A fish, he smells like a fish; a very ancient and
fish-like smell; A kind of not-of-the-newest poor-John.
A strange fish! Were I in England now, as once I was,
and had but this fish painted, not a holiday-fool there
but would give a piece of silver. There would this

30 *make a man*: make a man's fortune, *and*, pass for a man.

31 *doit*: coin of very small value.
32 *dead Indian*: Natives of the New World, alive or dead, were popular fairground exhibits in the sixteenth century.
33–4 *o'my troth*: upon my word.
35 *suffered*: perished.
37 *gaberdine*: cloak of coarse fabric.
40 *dregs*: Trinculo continues the metaphor he started with 'bombard'.

45 *swabber*: the seaman who washes down the decks.

52 *tailor . . . itch*: any wimp would serve to satisfy her sexual desire (tailors had a reputation for effeminacy).

56 *put*: play.
57 *men of Ind*: Indians.
58 *afeard*: frightened.
59–61 *As proper . . . ground*: as good a man who ever walked will not make him yield: Stephano adapts the proverbial phrase ('went on two legs').
62 *at' nostrils*: through his nose.

30 monster make a man—any strange beast there makes a man. When they will not give a doit to relieve a lame beggar, they will lay out ten to see a dead Indian. Legged like a man, and his fins like arms! Warm, o'my troth! I do now let loose my opinion, hold it no longer:
35 this is no fish, but an islander, that hath lately suffered by a thunderbolt. [*Thunder*] Alas, the storm is come again! My best way is to creep under his gaberdine—there is no other shelter hereabout. Misery acquaints a man with strange bed-fellows. I will here shroud till
40 the dregs of the storm be past.

He crawls under Caliban's *cloak*

Enter Stephano *singing, a bottle in his hand*

Stephano
I shall no more to sea, to sea,
Here shall I die ashore—
This is a very scurvy tune to sing at a man's funeral.
Well, here's my comfort. [*Drinks*]
[*Sings*]
45   The master, the swabber, the boatswain, and I,
            The gunner, and his mate,
        Lov'd Moll, Meg, and Marian, and Margery,
            But none of us car'd for Kate;
        For she had a tongue with a tang,
50   Would cry to a sailor, 'Go hang!'
        She lov'd not the savour of tar nor of pitch,
        Yet a tailor might scratch her where'er she did itch.
            Then to sea, boys, and let her go hang!
This is a scurvy tune too, but here's my comfort.

He drinks

Caliban
55 Do not torment me! O!
Stephano
What's the matter? Have we devils here? Do you put tricks upon's with savages and men of Ind? Ha? I have not scaped drowning to be afeard now of your four legs; for it hath been said, 'As proper a man as
60 ever went on four legs cannot make him give ground'; and it shall be said so again, while Stephano breathes at' nostrils.

Caliban

The spirit torments me! O!

Stephano

This is some monster of the isle with four legs, who
65 hath got, as I take it, an ague. Where the devil should
he learn our language? I will give him some relief, if
it be but for that. If I can recover him, and keep him
tame, and get to Naples with him, he's a present for
any emperor that ever trod on neat's-leather.

Caliban

70 Do not torment me, prithee! I'll bring my wood
home faster.

Stephano

He's in his fit now, and does not talk after the wisest.
He shall taste of my bottle. If he have never drunk
wine afore, it will go near to remove his fit. If I can
75 recover him and keep him tame, I will not take too
much for him; he shall pay for him that hath him,
and that soundly.

Caliban

Thou dost me yet but little hurt; thou wilt anon, I
know it by thy trembling. Now Prosper works upon
80 thee.

Stephano

Come on your ways. Open your mouth—here is that
which will give language to you, cat. Open your
mouth—this will shake your shaking, I can tell you,
and that soundly. [Caliban *drinks*] You cannot tell
85 who's your friend—open your chops again.

Trinculo

I should know that voice. It should be—but he is
drowned, and these are devils—O defend me!

Stephano

Four legs and two voices; a most delicate monster!
His forward voice now is to speak well of his friend,
90 his backward voice is to utter foul speeches and to
detract. If all the wine in my bottle will recover him,
I will help his ague. Come. [Caliban *drinks again*]
Amen! I will pour some in thy other mouth.

Trinculo

Stephano!

---

63 *torments me*: Trinculo's shivering gives
cause for Caliban's alarm.

65 *ague*: the shivering stage of a fever.

67 *recover*: cure.

69 *that . . . leather*: proverbial; 'neat's-
leather' = cowhide.

72 *after the wisest*: very sensibly.

74 *go near to*: do a lot to.
75-6 *I . . . much*: I will not sell him cheaply.

78 *anon*: presently.

81 *Come . . . ways*: come along with you.

84-5 *You . . . friend*: you don't know what's
good for you; perhaps Caliban did not
like his first taste of the liquor.
85 *chops*: jaws.

88 *delicate*: cunningly made.

91 *If . . . him*: even if it takes all the wine
in my bottle to cure him.

95 *call me*: address me.

97 *long spoon*: Stephano refers to the proverb, 'He must have a long spoon that will sup with the devil'.

104 *siege*: excrement.
105 *mooncalf*: monstrosity (thought to have been produced by the effect of the moon at its birth).
vent: defecate.

108 *overblown*: blown over, passed away.

112 *turn me about*: Trinculo perhaps seizes Stephano in a dance of joy.

114 *sprites*: spirits.

119 *sack*: white wine imported from Spain and Canary Islands.

124 *Here*: Stephano holds the bottle out to Trinculo for the swearing of his oath; he ignores Caliban until line 132.

Stephano

95 Doth thy other mouth call me? Mercy, mercy! This is a devil, and no monster. I will leave him; I have no long spoon.

Trinculo

Stephano! If thou beest Stephano, touch me, and speak to me; for I am Trinculo—be not afeard—thy

100 good friend Trinculo.

Stephano

If thou beest Trinculo, come forth. I'll pull thee by the lesser legs—if any be Trinculo's legs, these are they. [*Pulls him from under the cloak*] Thou art very Trinculo indeed! How cam'st thou to be the siege of

105 this mooncalf? Can he vent Trinculos?

Trinculo

I took him to be killed with a thunder-stroke. But art thou not drowned, Stephano? I hope now thou art not drowned. Is the storm overblown? I hid me under the dead mooncalf's gaberdine for fear of the

110 storm. And art thou living, Stephano? O, Stephano, two Neapolitans scaped!

Stephano

Prithee do not turn me about; my stomach is not constant.

Caliban

[*Aside*] These be fine things, an if they be not sprites.

115 That's a brave god, and bears celestial liquor. I will kneel to him.

Stephano

How didst thou scape? How cam'st thou hither? Swear by this bottle how thou cam'st hither—I escaped upon a butt of sack which the sailors heaved

120 o'erboard—by this bottle, which I made of the bark of a tree with mine own hands since I was cast ashore.

Caliban

I'll swear upon that bottle to be thy true subject, for the liquor is not earthly.

Stephano

Here; swear then how thou escaped'st.

Trinculo

125 Swum ashore, man, like a duck. I can swim like a duck, I'll be sworn.

128–9 *made like a goose*: i.e. with a long neck; Stephano comments on the length of Trinculo's drinking.

136 *when time was*: once upon a time.

138 *thy dog and thy bush*: According to popular superstition, the man was banished to the moon as punishment for gathering kindling on the sabbath day.

139 *the book*: Stephano continues to treat his bottle as a bible.

141 *this light*: i.e. the sun.
shallow: simple-minded.

143 *drawn*: drunk.

Stephano

Here, kiss the book. [*He gives* Trinculo *the bottle*] Though thou canst swim like a duck, thou art made like a goose.

Trinculo

130 O Stephano, hast any more of this?

Stephano

The whole butt, man. My cellar is in a rock by the seaside, where my wine is hid. How now, mooncalf, how does thine ague?

Caliban

Hast thou not dropped from heaven?

Stephano

135 Out o'th' moon, I do assure thee. I was the man 'i th' moon when time was.

Caliban

I have seen thee in her, and I do adore thee. My mistress showed me thee, and thy dog and thy bush.

Stephano

Come, swear to that: kiss the book. I will furnish it 140 anon with new contents. Swear.

Caliban *drinks*

Trinculo

By this good light, this is a very shallow monster. I afeard of him? A very weak monster! The man i' th' moon? A most poor, credulous monster! Well drawn, monster, in good sooth!

145 *I'll . . . island*: Caliban welcomes the strangers with the same hospitality that he originally showed to Prospero (1, 2, 337).

Caliban
145 I'll show thee every fertile inch o' th' island—and I
will kiss thy foot. I prithee be my god.
      Trinculo
By this light, a most perfidious and drunken
monster. When's god's asleep, he'll rob his bottle.
      Caliban
I'll kiss thy foot. I'll swear myself thy subject.
      Stephano
150 Come on, then, down and swear.
      Trinculo
I shall laugh myself to death at this puppy-headed
monster. A most scurvy monster! I could find in my
heart to beat him—
      Stephano
Come, kiss.
      Trinculo
155 —But that the poor monster's in drink. An
abominable monster!
      Caliban
I'll show thee the best springs; I'll pluck thee berries;
I'll fish for thee, and get thee wood enough.
A plague upon the tyrant that I serve!
160 I'll bear him no more sticks, but follow thee,
Thou wondrous man.
      Trinculo
A most ridiculous monster, to make a wonder of a
poor drunkard!
      Caliban
I prithee let me bring thee where crabs grow,

164 *crabs*: shellfish; it is unlikely that Caliban refers to the sour, inedible crabapples.
166 *jay's nest*: Caliban may be offering eggs from the hidden nest, but the jay was most prized for its plumage.
167 *marmoset*: a small monkey, common as a pet but also said to be edible.
168 *filberts*: hazelnuts.
169 *scamels*: This word is unknown—as is the creature it denotes, which must be either some rock-dwelling bird or a crustacean. (See 'Shakespeare's Sources', p. 90).
173 *him*: i.e. the bottle.

165 And I with my long nails will dig thee pig-nuts,
Show thee a jay's nest, and instruct thee how
To snare the nimble marmoset. I'll bring thee
To clust'ring filberts, and sometimes I'll get thee
Young scamels from the rock. Wilt thou go with me?
      Stephano
170 I prithee now lead the way without any more talking.
Trinculo, the king and all our company else being
drowned, we will inherit here. [*To* Caliban] Here,
bear my bottle. Fellow Trinculo, we'll fill him by and
by again.

Caliban

175 [*Sings drunkenly*] Farewell, master, farewell, farewell!

Trinculo

A howling monster; a drunken monster!

Caliban

No more dams I'll make for fish,
   Nor fetch in firing
   At requiring,
180 Nor scrape trenchering, nor wash dish:
   'Ban, 'Ban, Ca-Caliban
Has a new master—get a new man!
Freedom, high-day! High-day, freedom! Freedom,
   high-day, freedom!

Stephano

185 O brave monster! Lead the way!

[*Exeunt*

178 *firing*: firewood.

180 *trenchering*: Shakespeare's collective noun for 'trenchers' (= wooden platters).

182 *get a new man*: Prospero must find himself a new manservant.

183 *high-day*: holiday.

185 *brave*: fine.

Act 3

Act 3   Scene 1

Ferdinand labours patiently to obey
Prospero's orders whilst Miranda watches.
An unseen observer, Prospero listens with
satisfaction as they declare their love for each
other.

1–2 *their labour . . . set off*: the pleasure
  compensates for the pain.
3 *most poor*: even the poorest.
4 *mean*: lowly.
5 *but*: except that.
6 *quickens*: gives life to.
8 *crabb'd*: bad-tempered.

11 *sore*: strict.
13 *Had . . . executor*: was never performed
  by anyone like me.
  I forget: i.e. to do my work.
14–15 *these . . . do it*: Thoughts of Miranda
  come to Ferdinand's mind most
  powerfully when he is busiest at his
  work.

Scene 1

Enter Ferdinand *bearing a log*

Ferdinand
There be some sports are painful, and their labour
Delight in them set off; some kinds of baseness
Are nobly undergone; and most poor matters
Point to rich ends. This my mean task
5 Would be as heavy to me, as odious, but
The mistress which I serve quickens what's dead,
And makes my labours pleasures. O, she is
Ten times more gentle than her father's crabb'd,
And he's compos'd of harshness. I must remove
10 Some thousands of these logs and pile them up,
Upon a sore injunction. My sweet mistress
Weeps when she sees me work, and says such
    baseness
Had never like executor. I forget.
But these sweet thoughts do even refresh my labours,
15 Most busil'est when I do it.

Enter Miranda, *and* Prospero *at a distance, unseen*

Miranda
                              Alas, now pray you
Work not so hard. I would the lightning had
Burnt up those logs that you are enjoin'd to pile!
Pray set it down, and rest you. When this burns,
'Twill weep for having wearied you. My father
20 Is hard at study. Pray now, rest yourself;
He's safe for these three hours.

Ferdinand
                                        O most dear mistress,
The sun will set before I shall discharge
What I must strive to do.

Miranda
                              If you'll sit down
I'll bear your logs the while. Pray give me that;
25 I'll carry it to the pile.

Ferdinand
                              No, precious creature,
I had rather crack my sinews, break my back,
Than you should such dishonour undergo
While I sit lazy by.

Miranda
                              It would become me
As well as it does you, and I should do it
30 With much more ease, for my good will is to it,
And yours it is against.

Prospero
[*Aside*]   Poor worm, thou art infected!
This visitation shows it.

Miranda
                              You look wearily.

Ferdinand
No, noble mistress, 'tis fresh morning with me
When you are by at night. I do beseech you—
35 Chiefly that I might set it in my prayers—
What is your name?

Miranda
                              Miranda.—O my father,
I have broke your hest to say so.

19 *'Twill weep*: i.e. by exuding resin.

21 *safe*: safely occupied.

24 *the while*: meanwhile.

28 *become*: be as appropriate for.

31 *worm*: little thing; Prospero speaks affectionately.
32 *visitation*: charitable visit (see *2, 1, 12*) *and also* epidemic of the plague.

34 *When . . . night*: Ferdinand speaks with conventional hyperbole: the entire action of the play is completed within four hours.

37 *hest*: command.

37 *Admir'd Miranda*: Ferdinand puns on Miranda's name (= 'wonderful, to be wondered at').
39 *dearest*: most valuable.
   Full many a lady: a great many ladies.
40 *best regard*: close attention.
42 *diligent*: i.e. ready to listen.
   several: different, various.

45 *ow'd*: possessed.
46 *put it to the foil*: overthrew it.

48 *creature*: created being.

52–3 *How . . . of*: I have no knowledge of what people look like elsewhere.
53 *modesty*: maidenhood, virginity.
54 *dower*: dowry.

59 *condition*: rank.

61 *would not*: wish it were not.
62 *wooden slavery*: i.e. labouring to carry the wood.
63 *flesh-fly*: bluebottle, the fly that lays eggs on putrid flesh.
   blow: lay its eggs.

69 *kind event*: happy outcome.
70 *hollowly*: insincerely, falsely.
   invert: turn upside down.
71 *boded*: foretold.
   mischief: evil.

Ferdinand
                                    Admir'd Miranda,
Indeed the top of admiration, worth
What's dearest to the world! Full many a lady
40 I have eyed with best regard, and many a time
Th' harmony of their tongues hath into bondage
Brought my too diligent ear. For several virtues
Have I lik'd several women, never any
With so full soul but some defect in her
45 Did quarrel with the noblest grace she ow'd,
And put it to the foil. But you, O you,
So perfect and so peerless, are created
Of every creature's best.
        Miranda
                        I do not know
One of my sex, no woman's face remember,
50 Save from my glass, mine own; nor have I seen
More that I may call men than you, good friend,
And my dear father. How features are abroad
I am skilless of; but by my modesty,
The jewel in my dower, I would not wish
55 Any companion in the world but you;
Nor can imagination form a shape
Besides yourself to like of. But I prattle
Something too wildly, and my father's precepts
I therein do forget.
        Ferdinand
                    I am, in my condition,
60 A prince, Miranda; I do think a king—
I would not so!—and would no more endure
This wooden slavery than to suffer
The flesh-fly blow my mouth. Hear my soul speak:
The very instant that I saw you did
65 My heart fly to your service, there resides
To make me slave to it, and for your sake
Am I this patient log-man.
        Miranda
                            Do you love me?
        Ferdinand
O heaven, O earth, bear witness to this sound,
And crown what I profess with kind event
70 If I speak true; if hollowly, invert
What best is boded me to mischief: I,

72 *what*: whatever.

76 *breeds*: is developing.

77–81 *that dare . . . cunning*: Miranda
speaks innocent words whose sexual
undertones are barely suppressed.
79 *die*: The usual meaning of the word is
almost lost in the sense 'enjoy orgasm'.
want: lack—and desire.
81 *bashful cunning*: pretence of shyness.

84 *your maid*: (a) a virgin for your sake;
(b) your maidservant.

86 *mistress*: i.e. the lady who commands my
love; there are no implications, in this
usage, of illicit sexual relations.

88 *willing*: eager.
89 *of*: for.

90 *with . . . in't*: 'With heart and hand' was
a proverbial phrase.

91 *thousand-thousand*: i.e. 'Farewells'.

Beyond all limit of what else i' th' world,
Do love, prize, honour you.

Miranda
                                    I am a fool
To weep at what I am glad of.

Prospero
[*Aside*]   Fair encounter
75 Of two most rare affections! Heavens rain grace
On that which breeds between 'em!

Ferdinand
                              Wherefore weep you?

Miranda
At mine unworthiness, that dare not offer
What I desire to give, and much less take
What I shall die to want. But this is trifling,
80 And all the more it seeks to hide itself,
The bigger bulk it shows. Hence, bashful cunning,
And prompt me, plain and holy innocence!
I am your wife if you will marry me;
If not, I'll die your maid. To be your fellow
85 You may deny me, but I'll be your servant
Whether you will or no.

Ferdinand
                              My mistress, dearest,
And I thus humble ever.

                    He kneels

Miranda
My husband then?

Ferdinand
                              Ay, with a heart as willing
As bondage e'er of freedom. Here's my hand.

Miranda
90 And mine, with my heart in't. And now farewell
Till half an hour hence.

Ferdinand
                              A thousand-thousand!
[*Exeunt* Ferdinand *and* Miranda *separately*

Prospero

So glad of this as they I cannot be,
Who are surpris'd withal, but my rejoicing
At nothing can be more. I'll to my book,
95 For yet ere suppertime must I perform
Much business appertaining.

[*Exit*

93 *surprised withal*: taken unawares by all
this.

Act 3   Scene 2

Stephano and Trinculo, already drunk and
quarrelsome, listen to Caliban's plot to
murder Prospero—but they are overheard by
Ariel.

1 *Tell not me*: Trinculo has been trying to
moderate their drinking.
out: empty, finished.

2–3 *bear . . . board 'em*: get on with the
drinking; Stephano uses a nautical
expression (= sail up to and get aboard
an enemy vessel).

6 *brained like us*: have no more brains than
we have.

8 *set*: fixed (in a drunken stupor).

9 *brave*: fine.

12 *For my part*: as for me.

Scene 2

Enter Caliban, Stephano, *and* Trinculo

Stephano

[*To* Trinculo] Tell not me. When the butt is out, we
will drink water; not a drop before. Therefore bear
up and board 'em: servant-monster, drink to me.

Trinculo

Servant-monster! The folly of this island! They say
5 there's but five upon this isle: we are three of them;
if th'other two be brained like us, the state totters.

Stephano

Drink, servant-monster, when I bid thee. Thy eyes
are almost set in thy head.

Trinculo

Where should they be set else? He were a brave
10 monster indeed if they were set in his tail!

Stephano

My man-monster hath drowned his tongue in sack.
For my part, the sea cannot drown me: I swam, ere

I could recover the shore, five and thirty leagues off
and on, by this light. Thou shalt be my lieutenant-
15 monster, or my standard.
>   **Trinculo**
>   Your lieutenant if you list; he's no standard.
>   **Stephano**
>   We'll not run, Monsieur Monster.
>   **Trinculo**
>   Nor go neither; but you'll lie like dogs, and yet say
>   nothing neither.
>   **Stephano**
20   Mooncalf, speak once in thy life, if thou beest a good
>   mooncalf.
>   **Caliban**
>   How does thy honour? Let me lick thy shoe. I'll not
>   serve him, he is not valiant.
>   **Trinculo**
>   Thou liest, most ignorant monster: I am in case to
25   jostle a constable. Why thou debauched fish, thou,
>   was there ever man a coward that hath drunk so
>   much sack as I today? Wilt thou tell a monstrous lie,
>   being but half a fish and half a monster?
>   **Caliban**
>   Lo, how he mocks me! Wilt thou let him, my lord?
>   **Trinculo**
30   'Lord', quoth he? That a monster should be such a
>   natural!
>   **Caliban**
>   Lo, lo again! Bite him to death, I prithee.
>   **Stephano**
>   Trinculo, keep a good tongue in your head. If you
>   prove a mutineer, the next tree! The poor monster's
35   my subject, and he shall not suffer indignity.
>   **Caliban**
>   I thank my noble lord. Wilt thou be pleased to
>   hearken once again to the suit I made to thee?
>   **Stephano**
>   Marry, will I. Kneel and repeat it. I will stand, and
>   so shall Trinculo.

Enter Ariel, *invisible*

40 *As I told thee*: From this point onwards,
   Caliban speaks with more regular
   iambic rhythms.

Caliban
40 As I told thee before, I am subject to a tyrant, a
   sorcerer that by his cunning hath cheated me of the
   island.
Ariel
Thou liest.
Caliban
[*To* Trinculo] Thou liest, thou jesting monkey, thou!

45 *would*: wish.

45 I would my valiant master would destroy thee! I do
   not lie.
Stephano
Trinculo, if you trouble him any more in's tale, by
this hand, I will supplant some of your teeth.

48 *supplant*: displace, uproot.

Trinculo
Why, I said nothing.
Stephano

50 *Mum*: keep mum (= be silent).

50 Mum, then, and no more.—Proceed.
Caliban
I say by sorcery he got this isle;
From me he got it. If thy greatness will
Revenge it on him—for I know thou dar'st,
But this thing dare not—
Stephano
55 That's most certain.
Caliban
Thou shalt be lord of it, and I'll serve thee.
Stephano

57 *compassed*: achieved.

How now shall this be compassed? Canst thou bring
me to the party?
Caliban
Yea, yea, my lord. I'll yield him thee asleep,

60 *knock . . . head*: This would seem to
   recall the biblical episode of the murder
   of the sleeping Sisera by Jael (Judges 4:
   21).

60 Where thou mayst knock a nail into his head.
Ariel
Thou liest, thou canst not.

62 *pied ninny*: Caliban alludes to the
   jester's costume worn by Trinculo.
   patch: fool.

Caliban
What a pied ninny's this! Thou scurvy patch!
I do beseech thy greatness, give him blows,
And take his bottle from him. When that's gone,
65 He shall drink naught but brine, for I'll not show him

66 *quick freshes*: springs of fresh water
   (see *1*, *2*, *338*).

Where the quick freshes are.
Stephano
Trinculo, run into no further danger. Interrupt the

68–9 *turn . . . out o' doors*: have no mercy
on you; a servant was dismissed when
he was turned out of doors.

69 *stockfish*: piece of dried cod, beaten to
tenderize it for cooking.

monster one word further, and by this hand, I'll turn
my mercy out o' doors and make a stockfish of thee.

Trinculo

70 Why, what did I? I did nothing! I'll go farther off.

Stephano

Didst thou not say he lied?

Ariel

Thou liest.

Stephano

Do I so? Take thou that! [*Beats* Trinculo] As you like
this, give me the lie another time!

Trinculo

74 *give me the lie*: call me a liar.

75 I did not give the lie! Out o' your wits and hearing
too? A pox o' your bottle! This can sack and drinking
do. A murrain on your monster, and the devil take
your fingers!

76 *pox*: plague.
77 *murrain*: pestilence.

Caliban

Ha, ha, ha!

Stephano

80 Now forward with your tale. [*To* Trinculo] Prithee,
stand further off.

Caliban

Beat him enough. After a little time
I'll beat him too.

Stephano

Stand farther.—Come, proceed.

Caliban

85 Why, as I told thee, 'tis a custom with him
I' th' afternoon to sleep. There thou mayst brain him,
Having first seiz'd his books; or with a log

88 *paunch him*: stab him in the belly.
89 *weasand*: windpipe.

Batter his skull, or paunch him with a stake,
Or cut his weasand with thy knife. Remember

90 First to possess his books; for without them

91 *sot*: fool.

He's but a sot, as I am, nor hath not
One spirit to command—they all do hate him

93 *but*: only.

As rootedly as I. Burn but his books.

94 *brave utensils*: fine equipment (either
magical or household); the word is
stressed on the first syllable.

He has brave utensils, for so he calls them,

95 Which when he has a house, he'll deck withal.
And that most deeply to consider is
The beauty of his daughter. He himself

98 *nonpareil*: without equal.

Calls her a nonpareil. I never saw a woman

99 *dam*: mother.

But only Sycorax, my dam, and she;

100 But she as far surpasseth Sycorax
As great'st does least.

101 *brave*: good-looking.

102 *become*: be ideal.
103 *brood*: offspring.

115 *troll the catch*: sing the round.
116 *but whilere*: a little while ago.
117 *reason, any reason*: anything within reason.
119 *cout*: Like 'flout' and 'scout', this word must imply derision.
121 *Thought is free*: A proverbial saying.
122s.d. *tabor and pipe*: A combination of instruments associated with country festivities: the tabor was a small drum worn on the side of the body, and the tabor-pipe was played with one hand.

124–5 *the picture of Nobody*: i.e. nobody that I can see. The personification of 'Nobody' has a long history; the name was used, most memorably, by Ulysses to deceive the giant in the Cyclops episode of Homer's *Odyssey* (Book IX).

Stephano
                                              Is it so brave a lass?
Caliban
Ay, lord, she will become thy bed, I warrant,
And bring thee forth brave brood.
Stephano
Monster, I will kill this man. His daughter and I will
105 be king and queen—save our graces!—and Trinculo
and thyself shall be viceroys. Dost thou like the plot,
Trinculo?
Trinculo
Excellent.
Stephano
Give me thy hand. I am sorry I beat thee. But while
110 thou liv'st keep a good tongue in thy head.
Caliban
Within this half hour will he be asleep.
Wilt thou destroy him then?
Stephano
                                              Ay, on mine honour.
Ariel
This will I tell my master.
Caliban
Thou mak'st me merry. I am full of pleasure;
115 Let us be jocund. Will you troll the catch
You taught me but whilere?
Stephano
At thy request, monster, I will do reason, any reason.
Come on, Trinculo, let us sing.

                    [*They sing*]

        Flout 'em and cout 'em
120   And scout 'em and flout 'em
                Thought is free.
Caliban
That's not the tune.

                    Ariel *plays the tune on a tabor and pipe*

Stephano
What is this same?
Trinculo
This is the tune of our catch, played by the picture of
125 Nobody.

126–7 *If thou . . . list*: Stephano is drunk, and his bravado is confused: he orders the man to appear in his real shape ('likeness'), and will allow the devil to take his words in any way he wishes (i.e. as a challenge).

128 *forgive me my sins*: Trinculo is scared at the thought of the devil.

129–30 *Mercy upon us*: Stephano's courage collapses.

143 *my music for nothing*: This joke would be most appreciated when the play was performed at court, where the king regularly complained about the expense of court entertainment.

145 *I remember the story*: I haven't forgotten what we are going to do.

149 *lays it on*: is a good drummer.

Stephano
If thou beest a man, show thyself in thy likeness. If thou beest a devil, take't as thou list.

Trinculo
O, forgive me my sins!

Stephano
He that dies pays all debts. I defy thee! Mercy upon
130 us!

Caliban
Art thou afeard?

Stephano
No, monster, not I.

Caliban
Be not afeard, the isle is full of noises,
Sounds, and sweet airs, that give delight and hurt
    not.
135 Sometimes a thousand twangling instruments
Will hum about mine ears; and sometime voices,
That if I then had wak'd after long sleep,
Will make me sleep again, and then in dreaming
The clouds methought would open and show riches
140 Ready to drop upon me, that when I wak'd
I cried to dream again.

Stephano
This will prove a brave kingdom to me, where I shall
have my music for nothing.

Caliban
When Prospero is destroyed.

Stephano
145 That shall be by and by. I remember the story.

Trinculo
The sound is going away. Let's follow it, and after do
our work.

Stephano
Lead, monster, we'll follow. I would I could see this
taborer; he lays it on.

Trinculo
150 [*To* Caliban] Wilt come? I'll follow Stephano.

[*Exeunt*

Act 3   Scene 3

The king and his courtiers are weary and despondent. Whilst Prospero watches from a viewpoint high above the stage, they are further tormented by the appearance of a feast which, before they can enjoy it, vanishes from their sight. A strange apparition speaks to them, reproving their past conduct. Alonso admits his guilt, but Sebastian and Antonio are aggressive.

1   *By'r lakin*: by our ladykin, a mild form of the oath 'by our Lady'.

3   *forth-rights and meanders*: straight paths and winding ways.

5   *attach'd*: seized (a legal metaphor).

6   *dulling*: exhaustion.

7   *Even*: right.
    it: i.e. hope.

8   *flatterer*: deceiver.

10   *frustrate*: useless; the word is stressed on the first syllable.

12   *repulse*: setback—i.e. the sudden waking of the king and Gonzalo (*2, 1, 305*).

14   *throughly*: thoroughly.

Scene 3

Enter Alonso, Sebastian, Antonio, Gonzalo, Adrian, Francisco

Gonzalo

[*To* Alonso] By' r lakin, I can go no further, sir,
My old bones aches. Here's a maze trod indeed
Through forth-rights and meanders! By your
    patience,
I needs must rest me.

Alonso

                Old lord, I cannot blame thee,
5 Who am myself attach'd with weariness
To th' dulling of my spirits. Sit down and rest.
Even here I will put off my hope, and keep it
No longer for my flatterer. He is drown'd
Whom thus we stray to find, and the sea mocks
10 Our frustrate search on land. Well, let him go.

Antonio

[*Aside to* Sebastian] I am right glad that he's so out
    of hope.
Do not for one repulse forgo the purpose
That you resolv'd t' effect.

Sebastian

[*Aside to* Antonio]   The next advantage
Will we take throughly.

Antonio

[*Aside to* Sebastian]   Let it be tonight;

15 For now they are oppress'd with travail, they

Will not nor cannot use such vigilance

As when they are fresh.

Sebastian

[*Aside to* Antonio]   I say tonight. No more.

Solemn and strange music, and Prospero *on the top, invisible*

Alonso

What harmony is this? My good friends, hark!

Gonzalo

Marvellous sweet music!

Enter several strange shapes bringing in a banquet, and dance about it with gentle actions of salutations; and, inviting the king etc. to eat, they depart

Alonso

20 Give us kind keepers, heavens! What were these?

Sebastian

A living drollery! Now I will believe

That there are unicorns; that in Arabia

There is one tree, the phoenix' throne, one phoenix

At this hour reigning there.

Antonio

                        I'll believe both;

25 And what does else want credit, come to me,

And I'll be sworn 'tis true. Travellers ne'er did lie,

Though fools at home condemn 'em.

Gonzalo

                        If in Naples

I should report this now, would they believe me?

If I should say I saw such islanders—

30 For certes these are people of the island—

Who though they are of monstrous shape, yet note

Their manners are more gentle-kind than of

Our human generation you shall find

Many, nay almost any.

15 *now . . . travail*: now that they are fatigued with their efforts.

17s.d. *Prospero on the top*: Prospero is overseeing the action from the highest point of the stage, probably the musicians' gallery.

19s.d. *several*: various.
banquet: buffet of wine, fruit, and sweets.

20 *keepers*: guardian angels.
21 *living drollery*: live entertainment show.
23 *phoenix*: a mythical Arabian bird which lived alone and perched on a solitary tree: after one hundred years it expired in flames, and rose again from its own ashes.

25 *what . . . credit*: anything else that's unbelievable.
26 *Travellers . . . lie*: Travellers tales are notoriously incredible.
30 *certes*: certainly.
32 *gentle-kind*: well-bred.

36 *muse*: marvel.
39 *Praise in departing*: keep your praises
   until the end; a proverbial expression.
41 *viands*: food.
   stomachs: good appetites.
44 *mountaineers*: mountain-dwellers.
46 *Wallets*: wattles.
47 *heads . . . breasts*: In *Othello* Shakespeare
   also alluded to 'men whose heads Do
   grow beneath their shoulders'
   (*1*, 3, 144).
48 *putter-out of five for one*: Gonzalo's
   expression refers to a form of insurance
   available to travellers, who could
   deposit a sum of money with the broker
   before departing on their adventures;
   this would be repaid fivefold on their
   return with proof that the expedition
   had been successful.
49 *stand to*: set to work, begin eating.
52s.d. *Ariel . . . vanishes*: This episode is
   based on one of the experiences of
   Virgil's Aeneas and his Trojan
   companions (*Aeneid*, Book III). They
   had prepared a meal for themselves
   when a flock of harpies descended on
   the food, fouling and destroying it. The
   creatures were invulnerable, and would
   not depart until their leader had
   delivered a grim prophecy to Aeneas.
   harpy: The harpies were monsters with
   the wings and talons of birds, but with
   the faces of women.
   with a quaint device: by some ingenious
   mechanism.

Prospero

[*Aside*]   Honest lord,
35 Thou hast said well; for some of you there present
Are worse than devils.

Alonso

                    I cannot too much muse
Such shapes, such gesture, and such sound expressing,
Although they want the use of tongue, a kind
Of excellent dumb discourse.

Prospero

[*Aside*]   Praise in departing.

Francisco

40 They vanish'd strangely.

Sebastian

                    No matter, since
They have left their viands behind; for we have stomachs.
Will't please you taste of what is here?

Alonso

                                    Not I.

Gonzalo

Faith, sir, you need not fear. When we were boys,
Who would believe that there were mountaineers
45 Dewlapp'd like bulls, whose throats had hanging at 'em
Wallets of flesh?—or that there were such men
Whose heads stood in their breasts?—which now we find
Each putter-out of five for one will bring us
Good warrant of.

Alonso

                    I will stand to, and feed,
50 Although my last—no matter, since I feel
The best is past. Brother, my lord the duke,
Stand to and do as we.

Thunder and lightning

Enter Ariel, *like a harpy, claps his wings
upon the table, and with a quaint device the
banquet vanishes*

Ariel

You are three men of sin, whom Destiny,
That hath to instrument this lower world
55 And what is in't, the never-surfeited sea
Hath caus'd to belch up you, and on this island,
Where man doth not inhabit—you 'mongst men
Being most unfit to live. I have made you mad;
And even with such-like valour men hang and drown
60 Their proper selves.

Alonso, Sebastian, etc. draw their swords

You fools! I and my fellows
Are ministers of Fate—the elements
Of whom your swords are temper'd may as well
Wound the loud winds, or with bemock'd-at stabs
Kill the still-closing waters, as diminish
65 One dowl that's in my plume. My fellow ministers
Are like invulnerable. If you could hurt,
Your swords are now too massy for your strengths,
And will not be uplifted. But remember—
For that's my business to you—that you three
70 From Milan did supplant good Prospero,
Expos'd unto the sea, which hath requit it,
Him and his innocent child; for which foul deed,
The powers delaying, not forgetting, have
Incens'd the seas and shores, yea all the creatures
75 Against your peace. Thee of thy son, Alonso,
They have bereft; and do pronounce by me
Ling'ring perdition, worse than any death
Can be at once, shall step by step attend
You and your ways; whose wraths to guard you from,
80 Which here, in this most desolate isle, else falls
Upon your heads, is nothing but heart's sorrow,
And a clear life ensuing.

He vanishes in thunder. Then, to soft music,
enter the shapes again, and dance with mocks
and mows, and carrying out the table they
depart

Prospero

Bravely the figure of this harpy hast thou
Perform'd, my Ariel; a grace it had, devouring.

---

54 *to instrument*: as its instrument.

59 *such-like valour*: insane courage.
60 *proper*: own.

61–2 *the elements . . . tempered*: i.e. earth and fire: the swords are made from metal taken out of the earth and refined ('tempered') by the action of fire—but earth and fire have no power against wind and water.
62 *whom*: which.
63 *bemock'd-at*: derisory.
64 *still-closing*: closing as soon as they are parted.
65 *dowl*: filament, smallest part of a feather.
66 *like*: similarly.
67 *massy*: weighty.
71 *Expos'd*: The object of this verb is 'Him and his innocent child'.
requit it: avenged the deed.

76 *bereft*: bereaved, deprived.
77 *Ling'ring perdition*: gradual slow destruction.
77–8 *than . . . once*: than any sudden death can be.
79 *your ways*: everything you do.
whose wraths: i.e. the torments of 'Ling'ring perdition'.
80 *else*: otherwise.
81 *is nothing*: there is no alternative.
82 *clear*: blameless.
82s.d. *mocks and mows*: grimaces.

84 *devouring*: The word suggests that Ariel and his spirits may have removed the banquet by consuming it.

85   *bated*: omitted.

86–8   *so . . . have done*: Prospero praises the
rest of Ariel's actors for the spirited
performances they have all given, in
their different ways.

87   *observation strange*: unusual attention to
detail.

89   *knit up*: absorbed, enthralled.

93   *mine*: my.

95   *stare*: wonderment.

99   *bass my trespass*: sing out the depths of
my guilt in a bass voice. The waves and
winds have taken the higher parts in
this harmony of accusation.

100   *Therefore*: because of which (i.e. his
'trespass').

102   *But*: only.

103   *o'er*: one after another.

104   *desperate*: dangerously reckless.

106   *spirits*: vital powers.

108   *ecstasy*: frenzy.

85   Of my instruction hast thou nothing bated
In what thou hadst to say; so with good life
And observation strange my meaner ministers
Their several kinds have done. My high charms work,
And these, mine enemies, are all knit up
90   In their distractions. They now are in my power;
And in these fits I leave them, while I visit
Young Ferdinand, whom they suppose is drown'd,
And his and mine lov'd darling.   [*Exit above*

Gonzalo
I' th' name of something holy, sir, why stand you
95   In this strange stare?

Alonso
                                   O, it is monstrous, monstrous!
Methought the billows spoke and told me of it,
The winds did sing it to me; and the thunder,
That deep and dreadful organ-pipe, pronounc'd
The name of Prosper: it did bass my trespass.
100   Therefore my son i' th' ooze is bedded; and
I'll seek him deeper than e'er plummet sounded,
And with him there lie mudded.   [*Exit*

Sebastian
                                   But one fiend at a time,
I'll fight their legions o'er.

Antonio
                                   I'll be thy second.
[*Exeunt* Sebastian *and* Antonio

Gonzalo
All three of them are desperate: their great guilt,
105   Like poison given to work a great time after,
Now 'gins to bite the spirits. I do beseech you
That are of suppler joints, follow them swiftly,
And hinder them from what this ecstasy
May now provoke them to.

Adrian
                                   Follow, I pray you.
[*All exeunt*

Act 4

Prospero approves the efforts of Ferdinand, and rewards him with the gift of Miranda—but adds a stern warning! A masque arranged for the entertainment and instruction of the young lovers is interrupted when Prospero remembers the plot against his life. Caliban, Stephano, and Trinculo approach the magician's cell and find magic clothing.

1 *austerely*: severely.
  punish'd: disciplined.
3 *a third*: The other two 'thirds' of his life that Prospero values are, perhaps, his books and his kingdom.
4 *who*: whom.
5 *tender*: offer.
7 *strangely*: wonderfully.
11 *halt*: limp.

12 *Against an oracle*: even though an oracle were to contradict it.

14 *purchas'd*: won.
15 *break . . . knot*: destroy her virginity.
16 *sanctimonious*: sacred.

18 *aspersion*: sprinkling (of heavenly grace).

20–1 *bestrew . . . weeds*: Traditionally, the marriage-bed was strewn with flowers.
21 *loathly*: loathsome.
23 *As . . . light you*: in the way in which you want your marriage to go: torches were carried on the wedding day in honour of Hymen, the god of marriage, and (symbolically) to light the way for the bridal couple.
24 *fair issue*: fine children.
25 *murkiest den*: most darkly secluded cave.

Scene 1

Enter Prospero, Ferdinand, *and* Miranda

Prospero
[*To* Ferdinand] If I have too austerely punish'd you
Your compensation makes amends, for I
Have given you here a third of mine own life,
Or that for which I live; who once again
5 I tender to thy hand. All thy vexations
Were but my trials of thy love, and thou
Hast strangely stood the test. Here, afore heaven,
I ratify this my rich gift. O Ferdinand,
Do not smile at me that I boast of her,
10 For thou shalt find she will outstrip all praise,
And make it halt behind her.

Ferdinand
                I do believe it
Against an oracle.

Prospero
Then as my gift, and thine own acquisition
Worthily purchas'd, take my daughter. But
15 If thou dost break her virgin-knot before
All sanctimonious ceremonies may
With full and holy rite be minister'd,
No sweet aspersion shall the heavens let fall
To make this contract grow; but barren hate,
20 Sour-eyed disdain, and discord shall bestrew
The union of your bed with weeds so loathly
That you shall hate it both. Therefore take heed,
As Hymen's lamps shall light you.

Ferdinand
                As I hope
For quiet days, fair issue, and long life,
25 With such love as 'tis now, the murkiest den,

26 *opportune*: The word is stressed on the
    second syllable.
    suggestion: temptation.
27 *worser genius*: evil spirit. It was believed
    that every person was, at birth, allotted
    two spirits (the Christian 'angels') to be
    attendants and guardians throughout
    life.
    can: knows.
28 *to*: so as to.
29 *edge*: sharpness, ardour.
29–30 *that day's . . . When*: the celebration
    of that day on which.
30–1 *I shall . . . below*: Ferdinand will think
    that the wedding-night will never come
    either because the horses drawing the
    sun's chariot have collapsed
    ('foundered') through overwork, or
    because the night is forcibly prevented
    from coming.
33 *What*: come here.
35 *meaner fellows*: underlings.
37 *trick*: stunt, device.
    rabble: gang, mob.
39 *motion*: performance.

41 *vanity*: little nonsense (as opposed to
    the serious business of raising the storm
    and Ariel's meaningful presentation of
    the banquet).
42 *Presently*: immediately.

43 *with a twink*: in the twinkling of an eye
    (i.e. the time it takes to wink).

47 *mop and mow*: pulling funny faces; both
    words mean the same, i.e. 'grimace'.

50 *conceive*: understand.

51–2 *do not . . . rein*: don't allow yourselves
    to flirt too much; 'to give the rein' is to
    allow a horse to go as fast as it can.

The most opportune place, the strong'st suggestion
Our worser genius can, shall never melt
Mine honour into lust, to take away
The edge of that day's celebration
30 When I shall think or Phoebus' steeds are founder'd,
Or night kept chain'd below.

Prospero   Fairly spoke.
Sit then and talk with her, she is thine own.
What, Ariel! My industrious servant Ariel!

Enter Ariel

Ariel
What would my potent master? Here I am.
Prospero
35 Thou and thy meaner fellows your last service
Did worthily perform, and I must use you
In such another trick. Go, bring the rabble
O'er whom I give thee pow'r here to this place.
Incite them to quick motion, for I must
40 Bestow upon the eyes of this young couple
Some vanity of mine art: it is my promise,
And they expect it from me.
Ariel
                                    Presently?
Prospero
Ay, with a twink.
Ariel
Before you can say 'come' and 'go',
45   And breathe twice, and cry 'so, so',
Each one, tripping on his toe,
Will be here with mop and mow.
Do you love me, master? No?
Prospero
Dearly, my delicate Ariel. Do not approach
50 Till thou dost hear me call.
Ariel
                                    Well, I conceive.   [*Exit*
Prospero
[*To* Ferdinand] Look thou be true; do not give
    dalliance
Too much the rein. The strongest oaths are straw

53 *Be more abstemious*: don't indulge
   yourselves so much. Prospero perhaps
   objects to the present behaviour of
   Ferdinand and Miranda, who may be
   holding hands—or even kissing.
54 *good night*: i.e. that's the end of.
55–6 *The . . . liver*: my love is so utterly
   pure that it even cools my sexual ardour
   (which was thought to arise from the
   liver).
57 *a corollary*: a supernumerary, one too
   many.
58 *want*: lack.
   pertly: smartly.
59 *No tongue*: Silence was imperative for
   those present at magical demonstrations.
   All eyes: The courtly masques were
   primarily visual in their appeal, and
   Prospero's command emphasizes this
   aspect of his presentation.
59s.d. *Iris*: goddess of the rainbow and
   messenger of the gods (line 71). She
   introduces the masque, which is written
   mainly in rhymed couplets.
60 *Ceres*: goddess of the earth and
   patroness of agriculture.
   leas: meadows.
61 *vetches*: tares, grown for fodder.
62 *turfy*: turf-covered.
63 *stover*: winter forage.
64 *pioned and twilled*: These words,
   otherwise unknown, suggest that the
   river-banks have been shaped and
   strengthened to prevent erosion.
65 *hest*: command.
67 *dismissed bachelor*: rejected lover.
68 *being lass-lorn*: having lost his girl.
   poll-clipp'd: pollarded, pruned.
69 *marge*: margin, shore.
70 *air*: refresh.
   queen o'th' sky: Juno, queen of the gods.
72 *these*: i.e. the places just described.
73 *this grass-plot*: Iris perhaps indicates the
   stage, which would be covered with
   rushes.
74 *peacocks*: birds sacred to Juno, here
   drawing her chariot.
   amain: at high speed.
74s.d. It seems to have been a convention
   of the masque for the deity to appear
   suspended above the stage.
75 *entertain*: receive.
78 *saffron*: The description of Iris with
   saffron-coloured wings is taken from
   Virgil, *Aeneid* IV, line 700.

To th' fire i' th' blood. Be more abstemious,
Or else good night your vow.

Ferdinand

                    I warrant you, sir,
55 The white cold virgin snow upon my heart
Abates the ardour of my liver.

Prospero

                    Well.
Now come, my Ariel. Bring a corollary,
Rather than want a spirit. Appear, and pertly!

   Soft music

No tongue! All eyes! Be silent!

   Enter Iris

Iris

60 Ceres, most bounteous lady, thy rich leas
Of wheat, rye, barley, vetches, oats, and peas;
Thy turfy mountains, where live nibbling sheep,
And flat meads thatch'd with stover them to keep;
Thy banks with pioned and twilled brims,
65 Which spongy April at thy hest betrims
To make cold nymphs chaste crowns; and thy
     broom groves,
Whose shadow the dismissed bachelor loves,
Being lass-lorn; thy poll-clipp'd vineyard,
And thy sea-marge sterile and rocky-hard,
70 Where thou thyself dost air: the queen o' th' sky,
Whose watery arch and messenger am I,
Bids thee leave these, and with her sovereign grace,
Here on this grass-plot, in this very place,
To come and sport. Her peacocks fly amain.

          Juno's *chariot appears suspended above the*
          stage

75 Approach, rich Ceres, her to entertain.

   Enter Ariel *as* Ceres

Ceres

Hail, many-colour'd messenger, that ne'er
Dost disobey the wife of Jupiter;
Who with thy saffron wings upon my flowers
Diffusest honey-drops, refreshing showers;

81 *bosky*: covered with bushes.
unshrubb'd down: bare plains.
85 *estate*: bestow.
86 *bow*: rainbow.
87 *Venus*: the goddess of love.
her son: Cupid, the god of love, traditionally represented blindfolded, with bow and arrows.
as: so far as.
88–91 *Since . . . forsworn*: Ceres refers to the episode, narrated by Ovid in *Metamorphoses* V, when the god of the underworld, urged on by the powers of love, abducted her daughter, Proserpina, and kept her with him for six months of the year—during which time Ceres laid upon the earth the curse of winter.
89 *dusky*: gloomy, melancholy.
Dis: The Greek name for Pluto, god of the underworld.
92 *her deity*: her god-ship—Iris is irreverent.
93 *Cutting . . . Paphos*: speeding across the sky to her birthplace in Cyprus (which was the centre of her cult).
94 *Dove-drawn*: Doves were sacred to Venus, and drew her chariot.
95 *wanton charm*: spell to incite them to lust.
96–7 *that . . . lighted*: their marriage will not be consummated before the wedding ceremony; the 'bed-right'—or 'bed-rite'—is both debt and ritual.
98 *Mars's hot minion*: i.e. Venus, the lustful darling of Mars, the god of war.
99 *waspish-headed*: spiteful.
arrows: Cupid's arrows could sting love or hatred into the object of their aim.
100 *sparrows*: These were associated with Venus, and held to be emblematic of lechery.
101 *boy right out*: simply be a boy.
101–2 *Highest . . . Juno*: the most majestical queen; Juno was queen of the Roman gods and held particular responsibility for marriage.
102 *gait*: Whatever the disguise or means of transport, the true deity could always be discerned by her movement.

80 And with each end of thy blue bow dost crown
My bosky acres and my unshrubb'd down,
Rich scarf to my proud earth: why hath thy queen
Summoned me hither to this short-grass'd green?
    Iris
A contract of true love to celebrate,
85 And some donation freely to estate
On the bless'd lovers.
    Ceres
                    Tell me, heavenly bow,
If Venus or her son, as thou dost know,
Do now attend the queen? Since they did plot
The means that dusky Dis my daughter got,
90 Her and her blind boy's scandall'd company
I have forsworn.
    Iris
                Of her society
Be not afraid. I met her deity
Cutting the clouds towards Paphos, and her son
Dove-drawn with her. Here thought they to have done
95 Some wanton charm upon this man and maid,
Whose vows are that no bed-right shall be paid
Till Hymen's torch be lighted; but in vain.
Mars's hot minion is return'd again;
Her waspish-headed son has broke his arrows,
100 Swears he will shoot no more, but play with sparrows,
And be a boy right out.

    Ceres
                    Highest queen of state,
Great Juno comes; I know her by her gait.

    Juno's *chariot descends to the stage*

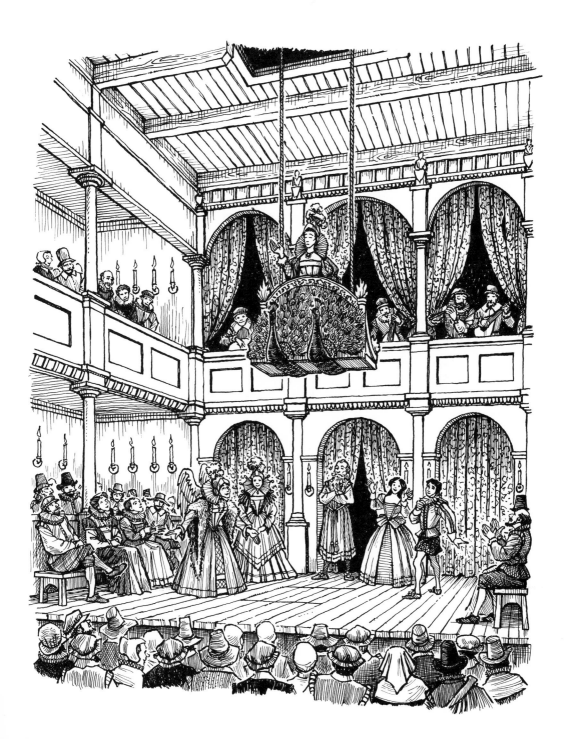

Juno

How does my bounteous sister? Go with me
To bless this twain, that they may prosperous be,
105 And honour'd in their issue.

> Ceres *joins* Juno *in the chariot, which rises
> and hovers above the stage. They sing*

Juno

Honour, riches, marriage-blessing
Long continuance, and increasing,
Hourly joys be still upon you!
Juno sings her blessings on you.

Ceres

110 Earth's increase, foison plenty,
Barns and garners never empty,
Vines with clust'ring bunches growing,
Plants with goodly burden bowing;
Spring come to you at the farthest,
115 In the very end of harvest!
Scarcity and want shall shun you;
Ceres' blessing so is on you.

Ferdinand

This is a most majestic vision, and
Harmonious charmingly. May I be bold
120 To think these spirits?

Prospero

                  Spirits, which by mine art
I have from their confines called to enact
My present fancies.

Ferdinand

              Let me live here ever.
So rare a wonder'd father and a wife
Makes this place paradise.

> Juno *and* Ceres *whisper, and send* Iris *on
> employment*

110 *foison*: abundance.

111 *garners*: granaries.
114–15 *Spring . . . harvest*: may spring return
    as soon as the harvest is over. Ceres in
    effect is revoking the curse of winter
    (see lines 88–91).
119 *Harmonious charmingly*: The word
    'charm' derives from the Latin *carmen*,
    which means both 'song' and 'spell'.
    May I be bold: would I be correct.
121 *their confines*: i.e. the natural elements
    they inhabit; the word is stressed on the
    second syllable.
122 *fancies*: fantasies.
123 *wonder'd*: able to create wonders.

124s.d. *employment*: Some stage business is
    called for here as Iris prepares to invoke
    the dancing nymphs and reapers.

Prospero

124 *Sweet*: The term of endearment may be addressed to Ferdinand or Miranda—or perhaps Prospero intends nothing more than 'Gently'.

128 *naiads*: water-nymphs.
windring: The word seems to be a compound of 'wandering' and 'winding'—but it could also be a very attractive misprint in the Folio text!

129 *sedg'd*: Sedge is a water plant.

130 *crisp*: rippling.

132 *temperate*: chaste; the naiads were associated with Diana, the virgin goddess.

134 *of August weary*: tired out with the hay-making work of August.

137 *fresh nymphs*: fresh-water naiads.
encounter: join.

138 *footing*: dancing.

> Sweet, now, silence!
> 125 Juno and Ceres whisper seriously.
> There's something else to do. Hush, and be mute,
> Or else our spell is marr'd.
>
> **Iris**
> You nymphs called naiads of the windring brooks,
> With your sedg'd crowns, and ever harmless looks,
> 130 Leave your crisp channels, and on this green land
> Answer your summons, Juno does command.
> Come, temperate nymphs, and help to celebrate
> A contract of true love. Be not too late.
>
> *Enter certain* nymphs
>
> You sunburn'd sickle-men, of August weary,
> 135 Come hither from the furrow and be merry;
> Make holiday; your rye-straw hats put on,
> And these fresh nymphs encounter every one
> In country footing.
>
> *Enter certain* reapers, *properly habited. They join with the* nymphs *in a graceful dance, towards the end whereof* Prospero *starts suddenly and speaks, after which, to a strange hollow and confused noise, they heavily vanish*

138s.d. *properly*: appropriately.
hollow: i.e. like an echo.
heavily: reluctantly, sorrowfully.

142 *avoid*: begone.

> **Prospero**
> [*Aside*] I had forgot that foul conspiracy
> 140 Of the beast Caliban and his confederates
> Against my life. The minute of their plot
> Is almost come. [*To the* spirits]—Well done, avoid.
> No more.
>
> Juno *and* Ceres *ascend in their chariot; exit* Iris
>
> **Ferdinand**
> This is strange. Your father's in some passion
> That works him strongly.

145 *distemper'd*: ill-tempered.

146 *mov'd sort*: distressed condition;
  Ferdinand's alarm remembers an earlier
  exhibition of Prospero's temper (*Act 1*,
  Scene 2) when he seemed to be its
  unwitting cause.

148 *revels*: entertainment: a formal
  indication that the masque is over and
  the audience must return to real life.

149 *foretold you*: told you earlier.

151 *baseless fabric*: structure with no
  foundation, nonsensical contrivance.

153 *the great globe itself*: Prospero's speech
  embraces also the Globe theatre, in
  which most of Shakespeare's plays were
  performed. See 'State of the art', p. xxv.

154 *which it inherit*: who inhabit there, *and
  who shall inherit it.*

155 *pageant*: display.

156 *rack*: wisp, cloud formation driven by
  wind—*and also* stage machinery for sky
  effects.

157 *on*: of.

158 *rounded*: surrounded, completed.

163 *beating*: agitated.

164 *I thank thee*: The words are addressed
  to Ferdinand and Miranda for their
  good wishes.

167 *presented*: played the part of.

Miranda
                              Never till this day
145 Saw I him touch'd with anger, so distemper'd.
    Prospero
    [*To* Ferdinand] You do look, my son, in a mov'd
      sort,
    As if you were dismay'd. Be cheerful, sir;
    Our revels now are ended. These our actors,
    As I foretold you, were all spirits, and
150 Are melted into air, into thin air,
    And, like the baseless fabric of this vision,
    The cloud-capp'd towers, the gorgeous palaces,
    The solemn temples, the great globe itself,
    Yea, all which it inherit, shall dissolve,
155 And, like this insubstantial pageant faded,
    Leave not a rack behind. We are such stuff
    As dreams are made on, and our little life
    Is rounded with a sleep. Sir, I am vex'd.
    Bear with my weakness, my old brain is troubled.
160 Be not disturb'd with my infirmity.
    If you be pleas'd, retire into my cell,
    And there repose. A turn or two I'll walk
    To still my beating mind.
        Ferdinand and **Miranda**
                              We wish your peace.
                                          [*Exeunt*
    Prospero
    Come with a thought!—I thank thee.—Ariel, come!

    Enter Ariel

    Ariel
165 Thy thoughts I cleave to. What's thy pleasure?
    Prospero
    Spirit, we must prepare to meet with Caliban.
    Ariel
    Ay, my commander. When I presented Ceres
    I thought to have told thee of it, but I fear'd
    Lest I might anger thee.
    Prospero
170 Say again, where didst thou leave these varlets?
    Ariel
    I told you, sir, they were red-hot with drinking,
    So full of valour that they smote the air

174 *bending*: aiming.
175 *tabor*: little drum.

176 *unback'd*: unbroken.
178 *As*: as if.
182 *filthy-mantled*: covered with filthy scum.
183 *that*: so that.
184 *O'er-stunk their feet*: Ariel communicates his disgust—but the precise sense of his words has never been determined.
186 *trumpery*: gaudy trash.
187 *stale*: decoy, bait.
188–9 *nature . . . stick*: A popular topic of Renaissance debate was the extent to which nurture—education and training—could transform nature in any essential way.
190 *Humanely*: See *1, 2, 346*.
192 *cankers*: rots from the inside.

193 *line*: lime-tree. At *5, 1, 10* Ariel refers to 'the line-grove which weather-fends [Prospero's] cell'.

197 *jack*: knave (as in a deck of cards).

For breathing in their faces, beat the ground
For kissing of their feet; yet always bending
175 Towards their project. Then I beat my tabor,
At which like unback'd colts they prick'd their ears,
Advanc'd their eyelids, lifted up their noses
As they smelt music. So I charm'd their ears
That calf-like they my lowing follow'd through
180 Tooth'd briars, sharp furzes, pricking gorse, and
        thorns,
Which enter'd their frail shins. At last I left them
I' th' filthy-mantled pool beyond your cell,
There dancing up to th' chins, that the foul lake
O'er-stunk their feet.
Prospero
                        This was well done, my bird.
185 Thy shape invisible retain thou still.
The trumpery in my house, go bring it hither,
For stale to catch these thieves.
Ariel
                        I go, I go.   [*Exit*
Prospero
A devil, a born devil, on whose nature
Nurture can never stick; on whom my pains,
190 Humanely taken, all, all lost, quite lost;
And as with age his body uglier grows,
So his mind cankers. I will plague them all,
Even to roaring.

Enter Ariel, *loaden with glistering apparel,
etc.*

Come, hang them on this line.

Prospero *and* Ariel *remain, invisible.*

Enter Caliban, Stephano, *and* Trinculo, *all
wet*

Caliban
Pray you tread softly, that the blind mole may not
195 hear a footfall. We now are near his cell.
Stephano
Monster, your fairy, which you say is a harmless fairy,
has done little better than played the jack with us.

Trinculo

Monster, I do smell all horse-piss, at which my nose
is in great indignation.

Stephano

200 So is mine. Do you hear, monster? If I should take a
displeasure against you, look you—

Trinculo

Thou wert but a lost monster.

Caliban

Good my lord, give me thy favour still.
Be patient, for the prize I'll bring thee to

205 Shall hoodwink this mischance; therefore speak
    softly,
All's hush'd as midnight yet.

Trinculo

Ay, but to lose our bottles in the pool!

Stephano

There is not only disgrace and dishonour in that,
monster, but an infinite loss.

Trinculo

210 That's more to me than my wetting; yet this is your
harmless fairy, monster!

Stephano

I will fetch off my bottle, though I be o'er ears for my
labour.

Caliban

Prithee, my king, be quiet. Seest thou here,

215 This is the mouth o' th' cell. No noise, and enter.
Do that good mischief which may make this island
Thine own forever, and I, thy Caliban,
For aye thy foot-licker.

Stephano

Give me thy hand. I do begin to have bloody

220 thoughts.

Trinculo

O King Stephano! O peer! O worthy Stephano—
look what a wardrobe here is for thee!

Caliban

Let it alone, thou fool, it is but trash.

Trinculo

O ho, monster! We know what belongs to a frippery.

He takes a robe from the tree and puts it on

203 The use of verse in Caliban's speech
now indicates some superiority over
Stephano and Trinculo, who are sinking
ever deeper into the moral mud.

205 *hoodwink this mischance*: make you close
your eyes to this accident.

212 *fetch off*: rescue.

221 *King Stephano*: Trinculo is reminded of
an old ballad:
    King Stephen was and a worthy peer,
    His breeches cost him but a crown;
    He held them sixpence all too dear,
    With that he called that tailor lown
    [lout] . . .

224 *what belongs to a frippery*: how to behave
in a second-hand clothes shop
('frippery').

225 O King Stephano!

Stephano

Put off that gown, Trinculo. [*Reaches for it*] By this hand, I'll have that gown.

Trinculo

Thy grace shall have it.

Caliban

The dropsy drown this fool! What do you mean
230 To dote thus on such luggage? Let't alone,
And do the murder first. If he awake,
From toe to crown he'll fill our skins with pinches,
Make us strange stuff.

Stephano

Be you quiet, monster. Mistress line, is not this my
235 jerkin? [*Removes it from the tree*] Now is the jerkin under the line. Now, jerkin, you are like to lose your hair, and prove a bald jerkin.

Trinculo

Do, do; we steal by line and level, an't like your grace.

Stephano

240 I thank thee for that jest: here's a garment for't.

> *He takes a garment from the tree and gives it to* Trinculo

Wit shall not go unrewarded while I am king of this country. 'Steal by line and level' is an excellent pass of pate.

> *He takes another garment and gives it to him*

There's another garment for't.

Trinculo

245 Monster, come put some lime on your fingers, and away with the rest.

Caliban

I will have none on't. We shall lose our time,
And all be turn'd to barnacles, or to apes
With foreheads villainous low.

Stephano

250 Monster, lay to your fingers. Help to bear this away where my hogshead of wine is, or I'll turn you out of my kingdom. Go to, carry this.

229 *dropsy*: a disease characterized by an excessive accumulation of fluid in the body—hence an insatiable desire to hoard anything.
230 *luggage*: paraphernalia, encumbrances.
233 *Make . . . stuff*: The line's emphasis is on 'us'.

235-7 *Now . . . jerkin*: Stephano's complicated wordplay involves 'under the line' = 'at the equator' *and* 'below the waist'; loss of hair could be due to the shipboard foolery—*or* to the treatment for syphilis.
238 *by line and level*: by plumb-line and carpenter's level—i.e. properly, according to rules.
an't like: if it please.

242-3 *pass of pate*: stroke of wit.

245 *put . . . fingers*: get your thieving fingers to work; birdlime was painted on trees to catch birds.

250 *lay to*: get working with.

Trinculo
And this.
Stephano
Ay, and this.

They give Caliban *the remaining garments.*
A noise of hunters heard. Enter divers spirits
in shape of dogs and hounds, hunting them
about, Prospero *and* Ariel *setting them on*

Prospero
255 Hey, Mountain, hey!
Ariel
Silver! There it goes, Silver!
Prospero
Fury, Fury! There Tyrant, there! Hark, hark!

Caliban, Stephano, *and* Trinculo *are*
driven out

Go charge my goblins that they grind their joints
With dry convulsions, shorten up their sinews
260 With aged cramps, and more pinch-spotted make
      them
Than pard or cat o' mountain.
Ariel
                                            Hark, they roar.
Prospero
Let them be hunted soundly. At this hour
Lies at my mercy all mine enemies.
Shortly shall all my labours end, and thou
265 Shalt have the air at freedom. For a little,
Follow, and do me service.
                                            [*Exeunt*

259   *dry convulsions*: spasmodic twitchings.
260   *aged cramps*: the cramps of old age.
        pinch-spotted: black and blue from being
        pinched.
261   *pard*: leopard.
        cat o' mountain: another name for
        leopard.
265   *at*: in.
266s.d. *Exeunt*: It is unusual for characters
        to leave the stage at the end of one
        scene only to return immediately for the
        beginning of another; here, however,
        the direction may well indicate that a
        short interval divided the play into two
        parts.

Act 5

Act 5   Scene 1

Prospero is now fully in command. When Ariel describes the condition of the king and courtiers, Prospero takes pity on them and, after a brief meditation on the achievements of his magical powers, releases them from his spell. He reveals himself for what he really is—the Duke of Milan—and extends his forgiveness to all. Alonso still grieves for his son—until Prospero draws a curtain and discloses Ferdinand and Miranda. Ariel escorts the crew of the king's ship from the scene of the shipwreck, and then drives in the drunken Stephano and Trinculo with Caliban to complete the picture. Prospero speaks the Epilogue.

1–2 Prospero uses the language of alchemy, a 'science' which aimed to transmute base metals (such as lead and iron) into gold.
project: design, experiment.
gather to a head: approach a critical point.
crack: blow up, fail.
2–3 *Time . . . carriage*: the time is up.

Scene 1

Enter Prospero *in his magic robes, and* Ariel

Prospero
Now does my project gather to a head.
My charms crack not, my spirits obey, and Time
Goes upright with his carriage. How's the day?

Ariel
On the sixth hour, at which time, my lord,
5 You said our work should cease.
     Prospero
                            I did say so
When first I rais'd the tempest. Say, my spirit,
How fares the king and's followers?
     Ariel
                          Confin'd together
In the same fashion as you gave in charge,
Just as you left them; all prisoners, sir,
10 In the line-grove which weather-fends your cell;
They cannot budge till your release. The king,
His brother, and yours, abide all three distracted,
And the remainder mourning over them,
Brimful of sorrow and dismay; but chiefly
15 Him that you term'd, sir, the good old Lord
    Gonzalo,
His tears runs down his beard like winter's drops
From eaves of reeds. Your charm so strongly works
    'em
That if you now beheld them, your affections
Would become tender.
     Prospero
                      Dost thou think so, spirit?
     Ariel
20 Mine would, sir, were I human.
     Prospero
                          And mine shall.
Hast thou, which art but air, a touch, a feeling
Of their afflictions, and shall not myself,
One of their kind, that relish all as sharply
Passion as they, be kindlier moved than thou art?
25 Though with their high wrongs I am struck to th'
    quick,
Yet with my nobler reason 'gainst my fury
Do I take part. The rarer action is
In virtue than in vengeance. They being penitent,
The sole drift of my purpose doth extend
30 Not a frown further. Go, release them, Ariel.
My charms I'll break, their senses I'll restore,
And they shall be themselves.

10 *line-grove*: grove of lime or linden trees.
   weather-fends: protects against the
   weather.

17 *eaves of reeds*: thatched roofs.

21 *touch*: sense.

23–4 *relish . . . they*: am fully as sensitive to
   suffering as they are.
24 *kindlier*: more in accordance with my
   [human] nature *and also* more
   generously.
25 *high wrongs*: great injuries.
   to th' quick: in my most sensitive part.
27–8 *The rarer . . . vengeance*: it is more
   noble to show compassion than to take
   revenge.
28 *virtue*: magnanimity.

33–50 *Ye elves . . . art*: Prospero's account of his magic powers is taken from a speech of the witch Medea in Ovid's *Metamorphoses* (see 'Shakespeare's Sources', p. 92).
standing lakes: still waters.

35 *fly*: flee from.

36 *demi-puppets*: the tiny doll-like creatures who have been at Prospero's command.

37 *green sour ringlets*: circles of sour grass, said to be caused by the fairies dancing—but actually the effect of nearby toadstools.

39 *midnight mushrooms*: mushrooms that grow up overnight.
that: you who.

40 *curfew*: The evening bell was rung at nine o'clock every night, signalling the end of the day—and the time when spirits and ghosts were free to walk, either until midnight or the first cock-crow.

41 *masters*: ministers, agents.

45 *rifted*: split.
oak: The oak, king of trees, was sacred to Jove (Jupiter), king of the classical gods.

46 *bolt*: thunderbolt.

47 *spurs*: roots.

50 *rough magic*: Prospero dismisses his achievements as mere conjuring tricks.

54 *airy charm*: music in the air.

57s.d. *Prospero observing*: Until he reveals himself at line 106, Prospero is wrapped in his magician's cloak and is invisible to the company assembled on stage.

Ariel

                          I'll fetch them, sir.
                                    [*Exit*

Prospero *traces a magic circle on the stage with his staff*

Prospero
Ye elves of hills, brooks, standing lakes, and groves,
And ye that on the sands with printless foot
35 Do chase the ebbing Neptune, and do fly him
When he comes back; you demi-puppets that
By moonshine do the green sour ringlets make,
Whereof the ewe not bites; and you whose pastime
Is to make midnight mushrooms, that rejoice
40 To hear the solemn curfew, by whose aid—
Weak masters though ye be—I have bedimm'd
The noontide sun, call'd forth the mutinous winds,
And 'twixt the green sea and the azur'd vault
Set roaring war; to the dread rattling thunder
45 Have I given fire, and rifted Jove's stout oak
With his own bolt; the strong-bas'd promontory
Have I made shake, and by the spurs pluck'd up
The pine and cedar. Graves at my command
Have wak'd their sleepers, op'd, and let 'em forth
50 By my so potent art. But this rough magic
I here abjure; and when I have requir'd
Some heavenly music—which even now I do—
To work mine end upon their senses that
This airy charm is for, I'll break my staff,
55 Bury it certain fathoms in the earth,
And deeper than did ever plummet sound
I'll drown my book.

Solemn music

Here enters Ariel *before; then* Alonso, *with a frantic gesture, attended by* Gonzalo; Sebastian *and* Antonio *in like manner, attended by* Adrian *and* Francisco. *They all enter the circle which* Prospero *had made, and there stand charmed; which* Prospero *observing, speaks*

58–9 *A solemn . . . fancy*: As therapy for the emotionally disturbed, music has been in use for centuries.
60 *boil*: i.e. which boil.

63 *ev'n sociable . . . thine*: in sympathy with the appearance of yours.
64 *Fall*: let fall.
   apace: quickly.

68 *clearer*: clearing.
69 *sir*: gentleman.
70 *graces*: favours.
71 *Home*: in full.

74 *pinch'd*: punished.

76 *whom*: i.e. who; Prospero's syntax changes in mid-sentence.

79–82 *Their understanding . . . muddy*: Prospero develops a metaphor of the understanding as a rising tide, which fills the shores of the reason and clears away the mud left at low tide.
82 *Not one*: there is not one.
84 *hat and rapier*: These were the essential accoutrements of an aristocrat's dress.

85 *discase me*: disrobe myself (of his magician's attire).
86 *sometime Milan*: before when I was Duke of Milan.
88–94 The music for Ariel's anticipatory song of freedom is printed on p. 102.
92 *After summer*: pursuing summer (like a migratory bird).

A solemn air, and the best comforter
To an unsettled fancy, cure thy brains,
60 Now useless, boil within thy skull. There stand,
For you are spell-stopp'd.
Holy Gonzalo, honourable man,
Mine eyes, ev'n sociable to the show of thine,
Fall fellowly drops. The charm dissolves apace,
65 And as the morning steals upon the night,
Melting the darkness, so their rising senses
Begin to chase the ignorant fumes that mantle
Their clearer reason. O good Gonzalo,
My true preserver, and a loyal sir
70 To him thou follow'st, I will pay thy graces
Home both in word and deed! Most cruelly
Didst thou, Alonso, use me and my daughter.
Thy brother was a furtherer in the act—
Thou art pinch'd for't now, Sebastian! Flesh and blood,
75 You, brother mine, that entertain'd ambition,
Expell'd remorse and nature, whom, with Sebastian—
Whose inward pinches therefore are most strong—
Would here have kill'd your king, I do forgive thee,
Unnatural though thou art.—Their understanding
80 Begins to swell, and the approaching tide
Will shortly fill the reasonable shore,
That now lies foul and muddy. Not one of them
That yet looks on me, or would know me. Ariel,
Fetch me the hat and rapier in my cell.

Exit Ariel *and returns immediately*

85 I will discase me, and myself present
As I was sometime Milan. Quickly, spirit!
Thou shalt ere long be free.

Ariel *sings, and helps to attire him*

Ariel
Where the bee sucks, there suck I,
In a cowslip's bell I lie;
90 There I couch when owls do cry;
On the bat's back I do fly
After summer merrily.

Merrily, merrily shall I live now
Under the blossom that hangs on the bough.

Prospero

95 Why, that's my dainty Ariel! I shall miss thee,
But yet thou shalt have freedom. [*Arranging his
attire*] So, so, so.
To the king's ship, invisible as thou art;
There shalt thou find the mariners asleep
Under the hatches. The master and the boatswain
100 Being awake, enforce them to this place,
And presently, I prithee.

Ariel

I drink the air before me, and return
Or ere your pulse twice beat.   [*Exit*

Gonzalo

All torment, trouble, wonder, and amazement
105 Inhabits here. Some heavenly power guide us
Out of this fearful country.

Prospero

                                        Behold, sir king,
The wronged Duke of Milan, Prospero.
For more assurance that a living prince
Does now speak to thee, I embrace thy body,

Embraces Alonso

110 And to thee and thy company I bid
A hearty welcome.

Alonso

                                        Whe'er thou beest he or no,
Or some enchanted trifle to abuse me,
As late I have been, I not know. Thy pulse
Beats as of flesh and blood; and since I saw thee,
115 Th'affliction of my mind amends, with which
I fear a madness held me. This must crave,
An if this be at all, a most strange story.
Thy dukedom I resign, and do entreat
Thou pardon me my wrongs. But how should
Prospero
120 Be living, and be here?

98–9 *There . . . hatches*: Ariel already knows this—it was he who gave the information to Prospero (1, 2, 230); but the reminder is valuable for the audience.

101 *presently*: immediately.

102 *I drink the air*: Ariel's promise of speed adapts a Latin phrase, *viam vorare*, meaning 'to devour the road'.

103 *Or ere*: before: the two words have the same meaning.

106 *fearful*: terrifying.

109 *embrace*: Ghosts and spirits are not susceptible to touch.

111 *Whe'er*: whether.

112 *enchanted trifle*: magic trick.
abuse: delude *and also* harm.

116 *crave*: call for.

117 *An . . . all*: if indeed this is true.

Prospero

[*To* Gonzalo]   First, noble friend,
Let me embrace thine age, whose honour cannot
Be measur'd or confin'd.

Embraces Gonzalo

Gonzalo

                              Whether this be,
Or be not, I'll not swear.

Prospero

                              You do yet taste

124 *subtleties*: deceptions.

Some subtleties o'th' isle, that will not let you
125 Believe things certain. Welcome, my friends all!

126 *brace*: pair.

[*Aside to* Sebastian *and* Antonio] But you, my brace
    of lords, were I so minded,
I here could pluck his highness' frown upon you,

128 *justify*: prove.

And justify you traitors. At this time
I will tell no tales.

Sebastian

[*Aside*]   The devil speaks in him!

Prospero

                                        No.
130 For you, most wicked sir, whom to call brother
Would even infect my mouth, I do forgive

132 *require*: request.
133 *perforce*: of necessity.

Thy rankest fault—all of them—and require
My dukedom of thee, which perforce I know
Thou must restore.

Alonso

                              If thou beest Prospero,
135 Give us particulars of thy preservation,
How thou hast met us here, whom three hours since
Were wreck'd upon this shore, where I have lost—
How sharp the point of this remembrance is!—
My dear son Ferdinand.

Prospero

                                        I am woe for't, sir.

Alonso

139 *woe*: sorry.

140 Irreparable is the loss, and patience
Says it is past her cure.

Prospero

                                        I rather think

142 *of*: by.

You have not sought her help, of whose soft grace

For the like loss I have her sovereign aid,
And rest myself content.

Alonso
                                    You the like loss?

Prospero
145 As great to me, as late; and supportable
To make the dear loss, have I means much weaker
Than you may call to comfort you, for I
Have lost my daughter.

Alonso
                                    A daughter?
O heavens, that they were living both in Naples,
150 The king and queen there! That they were, I wish
Myself were mudded in that oozy bed
Where my son lies. When did you lose your
      daughter?

Prospero
In this last tempest. I perceive these lords
At this encounter do so much admire
155 That they devour their reason, and scarce think
Their eyes do offices of truth, their words
Are natural breath; but howsoe'er you have
Been jostled from your senses, know for certain
That I am Prospero, and that very duke
160 Which was thrust forth of Milan, who most strangely
Upon this shore, where you were wreck'd, was landed
To be the lord on't. No more yet of this,
For 'tis a chronicle of day by day,
Not a relation for a breakfast, nor
165 Befitting this first meeting. Welcome, sir;
This cell's my court. Here have I few attendants,
And subjects none abroad. Pray you look in.
My dukedom since you have given me again,
I will requite you with as good a thing,
170 At least bring forth a wonder to content ye
As much as me my dukedom.

Here Prospero *discovers* Ferdinand *and*
Miranda *playing at chess*

Miranda
Sweet lord, you play me false.

Margin glosses:

145 *late*: recent.
146 *dear*: grievous.

150 *That*: provided that.
151 *mudded . . . bed*: lying in the same muddy sea-bed.

154–5 *do so . . . reason*: have so much to wonder at that their reason is swallowed up in amazement.
156 *eyes . . . truth*: they can believe their eyes.
156–7 *their words . . . breath*: they are speaking normally.
160 *strangely*: wonderfully.
163 *of day by day*: to be told in daily instalments.
164 *relation*: narrative.
for a breakfast: i.e. to be consumed as a quick meal.
167 *abroad*: elsewhere.
169 *requite*: repay.
171 s.d. *discovers*: reveals by drawing a curtain.
172 *you play me false*: you're cheating me.

Ferdinand
                                            No, my dearest love,
I would not for the world.
Miranda
Yes, for a score of kingdoms you should wrangle,
175 And I would call it fair play.
Alonso
                                            If this prove
A vision of the island, one dear son
Shall I twice lose.
Sebastian
                        A most high miracle!
Ferdinand
[*Coming forward*] Though the seas threaten, they
      are merciful.
I have curs'd them without cause.

He kneels before Alonso

Alonso
                                            Now all the blessings
180 Of a glad father compass thee about!
Arise, and say how thou cam'st here.

Ferdinand *rises*

Miranda
                                            O wonder!
How many goodly creatures are there here!
How beauteous mankind is! O brave new world
That has such people in't!
Prospero
                                    'Tis new to thee.
Alonso
185 What is this maid with whom thou wast at play?
Your eld'st acquaintance cannot be three hours.
Is she the goddess that hath sever'd us,
And brought us thus together?
Ferdinand
                                            Sir, she is mortal;
But by immortal providence, she's mine.
190 I chose her when I could not ask my father
For his advice—nor thought I had one. She
Is daughter to this famous Duke of Milan,
Of whom so often I have heard renown,

174 *a score of kingdoms*: Miranda contradicts
      Ferdinand's grand assertion.
      wrangle: dispute.

176 *vision*: illusion.
177 *A . . . miracle*: Sebastian is impressed—
      or perhaps merely sarcastic.

183 *mankind*: the race of men; Miranda
      probably means 'humankind', although
      she has not yet seen another woman.

186 *eld'st*: longest.
187 *goddess*: Ferdinand also assumed that
      Miranda was a goddess (*1*, 2, 422).

But never saw before; of whom I have
195 Receiv'd a second life; and second father
This lady makes him to me.

Alonso
                                    I am hers.
But O, how oddly will it sound that I
Must ask my child forgiveness!

Prospero
                                There, sir, stop.
Let us not burden our remembrances with
200 A heaviness that's gone.

Gonzalo
                                    I have inly wept,
Or should have spoke ere this: look down, you gods,
And on this couple drop a blessed crown;
For it is you that have chalk'd forth the way
Which brought us hither.

Alonso
                                I say 'amen', Gonzalo.

Gonzalo
205 Was Milan thrust from Milan that his issue
Should become kings of Naples? O rejoice
Beyond a common joy, and set it down
With gold on lasting pillars! In one voyage
Did Claribel her husband find at Tunis,
210 And Ferdinand, her brother, found a wife
Where he himself was lost, Prospero his dukedom
In a poor isle, and all of us ourselves
When no man was his own.

Alonso
[*To* Ferdinand *and* Miranda] Give me your hands.
Let grief and sorrow still embrace his heart
215 That doth not wish you joy!

Gonzalo
                                Be it so, amen.

Enter Ariel, *with the* Master *and* Boatswain
amazedly following

O look, sir, look, sir, here is more of us!
I prophesied if a gallows were on land
This fellow could not drown. [*To* Boatswain] Now,
     blasphemy,

196 *I am hers*: I am her father—just as Prospero has become 'father' to Ferdinand.

199–200 *Let . . . gone*: let's forget all this sadness which is now in the past.

203 *chalk'd forth*: marked out (as with chalk).

205 *Milan . . . Milan*: the Duke of Milan . . . the dukedom of Milan.

208 *lasting pillars*: permanent monuments.

212 *all of us*: Gonzalo seems to forget Antonio and Sebastian.
213 *his own*: in control of himself.
214 *still*: forever.
217 *I prophesied*: i.e. in *Act 1*, Scene 1.
218 *blasphemy*: It was Sebastian who accused the Boatswain of blasphemy in the play's first scene (line 39).

219 *swear'st grace o'erboard*: drives God's
grace overboard by swearing.
220 *no mouth*: nothing to say.

223 *three glasses since*: three hours ago (the
running of three hour-glasses).
gave out: declared.
224 *yare*: trim, seaworthy.

226 *tricksy spirit*: clever little spirit.

227 *strengthen*: grow.

230 *of sleep*: asleep.

232 *but even now*: only just now.
several: sundry.

236 *in all our trim*: properly dressed.

238 *Cap'ring*: dancing for joy.
on a trice: in an instant.
240 *moping*: bewildered.

242 *maze*: Alonso echoes Gonzalo's
description of the island, 'Here's a maze
trod indeed' (3, 3, 2).
244 *conduct*: manager, director.

246 *infest*: trouble.
beating on: hammering out.
247 *At pick'd leisure*: when we can find some
spare time.

That swear'st grace o'erboard, not an oath on shore?
220 Hast thou no mouth by land? What is the news?
Boatswain
The best news is that we have safely found
Our king and company; the next, our ship,
Which but three glasses since we gave out split,
Is tight and yare and bravely rigg'd as when
225 We first put out to sea.
Ariel
[*Aside to* Prospero]   Sir, all this service
Have I done since I went.
Prospero
[*Aside to* Ariel]   My tricksy spirit!
Alonso
These are not natural events, they strengthen
From strange to stranger. Say, how came you hither?
Boatswain
If I did think, sir, I were well awake,
230 I'd strive to tell you. We were dead of sleep,
And—how we know not—all clapp'd under hatches,
Where but even now with strange and several noises
Of roaring, shrieking, howling, jingling chains,
And more diversity of sounds, all horrible,
235 We were awak'd, straightway at liberty,
Where we, in all our trim, freshly beheld
Our royal, good, and gallant ship; our master
Cap'ring to eye her—on a trice, so please you,
Even in a dream, were we divided from them,
240 And were brought moping hither.
Ariel
[*Aside to* Prospero]   Was't well done?
Prospero
[*Aside to* Ariel] Bravely, my diligence. Thou shalt be
free.
Alonso
This is as strange a maze as e'er men trod,
And there is in this business more than nature
Was ever conduct of. Some oracle
245 Must rectify our knowledge.
Prospero
    Sir, my liege,
Do not infest your mind with beating on
The strangeness of this business. At pick'd leisure,

248 *single*: uninterrupted.

249 *Which . . . probable*: with an explanation that you will find convincing ('probable' = capable of proof).

250 *happen'd accidents*: events that have occurred.

Which shall be shortly single, I'll resolve you,
Which to you shall seem probable, of every
250 These happen'd accidents; till when, be cheerful
And think of each thing well. [*Aside to* Ariel] Come
          hither, spirit.
Set Caliban and his companions free;
Untie the spell.   [*Exit* Ariel
          How fares my gracious sir?
There are yet missing of your company
255 Some few odd lads that you remember not.

          Enter Ariel, *driving in* Caliban, Stephano,
          and Trinculo *in their stolen apparel*

Stephano
Every man shift for all the rest, and let no man take
care for himself, for all is but fortune. Coraggio,
bully-monster, coraggio!

256–7 *Every . . . himself*: Stephano means just the opposite!

257 *Coraggio*: courage (Italian).

Trinculo
If these be true spies which I wear in my head, here's
260 a goodly sight.

259 *If . . . head*: if my eyes can be believed.

261 *Setebos*: Caliban's god (see *1, 2, 372*). *brave*: splendid.

266 *plain fish*: Antonio's first reaction to Caliban is like that of Trinculo (*2, 2, 24*).

267 *badges*: although they are carrying the clothes stolen from Prospero, Stephano and Trinculo are still wearing the insignia of Alonso's servants.

Caliban
O Setebos, these be brave spirits indeed.
How fine my master is! I am afraid
He will chastise me.

Sebastian
                    Ha, ha!
What things are these, my lord Antonio?
265 Will money buy 'em?

Antonio
                    Very like. One of them
Is a plain fish, and no doubt marketable.

Prospero
Mark but the badges of these men, my lords,
Then say if they be true. This misshapen knave,
His mother was a witch, and one so strong

268 *true*: honest.

270 *control the moon*: Sycorax apparently shared, with Prospero, some of the powers of Medea, the witch of Ovid's *Metamorphoses*; see above, lines 33–50.

271 *without*: beyond the boundaries of.

272 *demi-devil*: Prospero repeats his charge of *1, 2, 319–20* that Caliban was 'got by the devil himself'.

275 *own*: acknowledge.

270 That could control the moon, make flows and ebbs,
And deal in her command without her power.
These three have robb'd me, and this demi-devil—
For he's a bastard one—had plotted with them
To take my life. Two of these fellows you
275 Must know and own; this thing of darkness I
Acknowledge mine.

Caliban

                    I shall be pinch'd to death!

Alonso

Is not this Stephano, my drunken butler?

Sebastian

He is drunk now—where had he wine?

Alonso

279 *reeling-ripe*: ready (i.e. drunk enough) to reel about.

And Trinculo is reeling-ripe! Where should they

280 Find this grand liquor that hath gilded 'em?

280 *gilded*: flushed their faces.

How cam'st thou in this pickle?

281 *pickle*: predicament—*and also* preserving liquid.

Trinculo

I have been in such a pickle since I saw you last that

282 *such a pickle*: Trinculo refers to the 'foul lake' into which he was led (*4, 1, 182*).

I fear me will never out of my bones. I shall not fear

284 *fly-blowing*: i.e. because he is thoroughly pickled and preserved.

fly-blowing.

Sebastian

285 Why, how now, Stephano?

Stephano

O, touch me not; I am not Stephano, but a cramp.

Prospero

287 *sirrah*: The term expresses contempt.

You'd be king o' the isle, sirrah?

Stephano

I should have been a sore one then.

Alonso

[*Indicating* Caliban] This is a strange thing as e'er I

look'd on.

Prospero

290 *manners*: conduct *and* moral character.

290 He is as disproportion'd in his manners

As in his shape. Go, sirrah, to my cell;

292 *look*: hope.

Take with you your companions. As you look

293 *trim it handsomely*: make a good job of decorating it.

To have my pardon, trim it handsomely.

Caliban

Ay, that I will; and I'll be wise hereafter,

295 *grace*: forgiveness and favour.

295 And seek for grace. What a thrice-double ass

Was I to take this drunkard for a god,

And worship this dull fool!

Prospero

                    Go to, away.

Alonso

298 *luggage*: i.e. the stolen garments (*4, 1, 230*).

Hence, and bestow your luggage where you found it.

Sebastian

Or stole it, rather.

                    [*Exeunt* Caliban, Stephano, *and* Trinculo

Prospero

300 Sir, I invite your highness and your train
To my poor cell, where you shall take your rest
For this one night, which part of it I'll waste
With such discourse as I not doubt shall make it
Go quick away: the story of my life,
305 And the particular accidents gone by
Since I came to this isle; and in the morn
I'll bring you to your ship, and so to Naples,
Where I have hope to see the nuptial
Of these our dear-belov'd solemnized,
310 And thence retire me to my Milan, where
Every third thought shall be my grave.

Alonso

                                        I long
To hear the story of your life, which must
Take the ear strangely.

Prospero

                              I'll deliver all,
And promise you calm seas, auspicious gales,
315 And sail so expeditious that shall catch
Your royal fleet far off. My Ariel, chick,
That is thy charge. Then to the elements
Be free, and fare thou well.—Please you draw near.

                                        [*Exeunt* all

302 *waste*: take up, occupy.

305 *accidents*: events.

307 *bring*: accompany.

309 *solemnized*: The word is stressed on the second and fourth syllables.

313 *deliver*: relate.

315 *sail*: a sailing.
316 *far off*: Alonso's ship was separated from the rest of his fleet by Prospero's tempest, and the other ships are now several hours further ahead.
318 *draw near*: come inside.

Epilogue

Prospero addresses the audience, speaking to
them not as an actor who has just performed
his part but as a character with a future that
lies beyond the stage and the world of the
play.

327 *bands*: bonds.
328 *hands*: Sudden noises, and especially the
clapping of hands, were thought to
dissolve spells.
329 *Gentle breath*: kind words (i.e. about the
play).
330 *project*: enterprise, scheme—see 5, 1, 1.
331 *want*: lack.

335 *pierces*: i.e. in contrast to the 'gentle
breath' of line 329.
336 *Mercy*: i.e. God himself.
    frees: frees from.
338 *indulgence*: leniency of judgement—*and
also*, remission of punishment for sin.

Epilogue

Prospero

Now my charms are all o'erthrown,
320 And what strength I have's mine own,
Which is most faint. Now 'tis true
I must be here confin'd by you,
Or sent to Naples. Let me not,
Since I have my dukedom got,
325 And pardon'd the deceiver, dwell
In this bare island by your spell,
But release me from my bands
With the help of your good hands.
Gentle breath of yours my sails
330 Must fill, or else my project fails,
Which was to please. Now I want
Spirits to enforce, art to enchant;
And my ending is despair
Unless I be reliev'd by prayer,
335 Which pierces so that it assaults
Mercy itself, and frees all faults.
As you from crimes would pardon'd be,
Let your indulgence set me free.   [*Exit*

Shakespeare's Sources

A. The wreck and redemption of the *Sea-Adventure*

In May 1609, a fleet of nine ships set sail for Virginia with five hundred colonists, but on 25 July the vessel holding the leaders, Gates and Summers, was separated from the others by a sudden storm. Being near the coast of the Bermudas, the crew were forced to run their ship towards the shore, where it was locked between two rocks. The crew, with most of the ship's fittings and stores, got ashore safely, but it was another year, May 1610, before they were able to join the main body of the colonists in Virginia. News of the storm had arrived in England before the end of 1609, and it was believed that the ship, the *Sea-Adventure*, had perished with all hands aboard. Shakespeare was acquainted with members of the Virginia Company—such as the Earls of Pembroke and Southampton, who were both financially interested in the plantation—and must have been able to read the original letter in which William Strachey, reporting back to the Company, described the strange experiences of the shipwrecked colonists. His was not the only account: there are several others, which vary only in detail, but Strachey's is the most comprehensive.

> A true repertory of the wreck and redemption of Sir Thomas Gates, Knight, upon and from the islands of the Bermudas . . .
> July 15, 1610, written by William Strachey, Esquire.

With graphic detail, Strachey describes a fearful tempest which raged from Monday to Friday in 'a restless tumult . . . so exceedingly as we could not apprehend in our imaginations any possibility of greater violence . . . not only more terrible, but more constant, fury added to fury, and one storm urging a second more outrageous than the former'. The confusions of winds and thunder were augmented by the distress of the passengers, 'not used to such hurly and discomforts', but the 'clamours [were] drowned in the winds, and the winds in the thunder. Prayers might well be in the heart and lips, but drowned in the outcries of the officers: nothing heard that could give comfort, nothing seen that might encourage hope.'

Thursday night brought a new terror in the apparition of 'a little round light, like a faint star, trembling and streaming along with a sparkling blaze, half the height upon the main mast, and shooting sometimes from shroud to shroud: and for three hours together, or rather more, half the night it kept with us, running sometimes along the main-yard to the very end, and then returning'. Strachey knew that such phenomena were 'usual' in Mediterranean storms, although 'the superstitious seamen make many constructions of this sea-fire', the Italians calling it 'a sacred body, *corpo sancto*', and the Spaniards 'St Elmo'. However, he adds ruefully, 'it did not light us any whit'.

The mariners continued to wrestle with the elements: ' . . . East and by south we steered away as much as we could bear upright, which was no small carefulness nor pain to do, albeit we much unrigged our ship, threw overboard much luggage, many a trunk and chest . . . and staved in many a butt of beer, hogsheads of oil, wine, and vinegar.'

[By Friday morning] ' . . . it wanted but little but that there had been a general determination to have shut up hatches and, commending our sinful souls to God, committed the ship to the mercy of the sea' when suddenly, through 'the goodness and sweet introduction of better hope by our merciful God given unto us', land was sighted. Skilful navigation brought the ship safely ashore, although the landing was on 'the dangerous and dreaded' islands of the Bermudas, which 'are often afflicted and rent with tempests, great strokes of thunder, lightning, and rain in the extremity of violence'.

Strachey proceeds to refute the 'foul and general error' that these islands 'can be no habitation for men, but rather given over to devils and wicked spirits'. On the contrary, he assures his readers, 'we find them now by experience to be as habitable and commodious as most countries of the same climate and situation . . . The soil of the whole island is one and the same, the mould dark, red, sandy, dry.' Cultivation of crops was easy because, although there were 'no rivers or running springs of fresh water', there was underground water which could be trapped in 'fishing pools or standing pools continually'. The seashore offered a plentiful supply of fish, and crustaceans—crayfish, crabs, oysters, and whelks—were to be taken 'from under broken rocks'. Among various other wildfowl was one 'web-footed fowl . . . of the bigness of an English green plover or sea-mew',[1] and the colonists found that the tortoise

---

[1]   Could this have been the origin of Caliban's 'scamels' (2, 2, 169)?

was 'a reasonable toothsome (some say) wholesome meat . . . such a kind of meat as man can neither absolutely call fish nor flesh'.

Having survived the wreck, however, the colonists encountered a new danger—dissension among the settlers: 'faction and conjuration afoot, deadly and bloody, in which the life of our governor, with many others, were threatened'. The insurrection was quickly detected ('all giddy and lawless attempts have always something of imperfection'), and eventually the party was able to leave the island and resume their voyage to Virginia where they found a land which was fertile but 'full of misery and misgovernment'. One of the settlers was captured by the Indians and sacrificed to their god, and this 'did not a little trouble the lieutenant-governor, who since his first landing in the country, how justly soever provoked, would not by any means be wrought to a violent proceeding against them for all the practices of villainy with which they daily endangered our men, thinking it possible by a more tractable course to win them to a better condition; but now, being startled by this, he well perceived how little a fair and noble entreaty works upon a barbarous disposition, and therefore in some measure purposed to be revenged'.

Strachey's conclusion is that 'the permissive providence of God' had been 'the ground of all those miseries', permitting 'the forementioned violent storm', the dispersion of the fleet, and the shipwreck 'in those infortunate (yet fortunate) islands'. He quotes from the Virginia Company's pamphlet, *A True Declaration of Virginia*, 'A colony is therefore denominated because they should be *coloni*, tillers of the earth and stewards of fertility', and adds his own comment on the 'idleness' of the mutineers and the natives: '*Dii laboribus omnia vendunt*, God sells us all things for our labour, when Adam himself might not live in paradise without dressing the garden'.

(Published in *Purchas his Pilgrimes* (1625), part 4, book 9, chapter 6)

B. *The Essays of Michel de Montaigne*, translated by John Florio (1603)

Gonzalo's Utopia, Act 2, Scene 1, lines 144–65

. . . It is a nation [among the cannibals] . . . that hath no kind of traffic, no knowledge of letters, no intelligence of numbers, no name of magistrate, nor of politic superiority; no use of service, of riches or of poverty; no contracts, no successions, no partitions, no occupation but idle; no respect of kindred, but common, no apparel but natural, no manuring of lands, no use of wine, corn, or mettle. The very words that import lying, falsehood, treason, dissimulation, covetousness, envy, detraction, and pardon, were never heard of amongst them . . .

('Of the Cannibals')

Prospero's 'rarer virtue', Act 5, Scene 1, lines 27–8

. . . He that through a natural facility and genuine mildness should neglect or contemn injuries received should no doubt perform a rare action, and worthy commendation. But he who, being touched and stung to the quick with any wrong or offence received, should arm himself with reason against this furiously-blind desire of revenge, and in the end, after a great conflict, yield himself master over it, should doubtless do much more. The first should do well, the other virtuously: the one action might be termed goodness, the other virtue. For it seemeth the very name of virtue presupposeth difficulty, and inferreth resistance, and cannot well exercise itself without an enemy.

('Of Cruelty')

C. Ovid's *Metamorphoses, Book VII, lines 197–209*

Medea addresses her agents:

'. . . ye elves of hills, of brooks, of woods alone,
Of standing lakes, and of the night, approach ye every one,
Through help of whom (the crooked banks much wond'ring at
   the thing)
I have compelled streams to run clean backward to their spring.
By charms I make the calm seas rough and make the rough seas
   plain,
And cover all the sky with clouds, and chase them thence again.
By charms I raise and lay the winds, and burst the viper's jaw,
And from the bowels of the earth both stones and trees do draw.
Whole woods and forests I remove; I make the mountains shake,
And even the earth itself to groan and fearfully to quake.
I call up dead men from their graves; and thee, O lightsome moon,
I darken oft, though beaten brass abate thy peril soon;
Our sorcery dims the morning fair and darks the sun at noon . . .'

Golding translates these Latin lines:

> . . . auraeque et venti montesque amnesque lacusque
> dique omnes nemorum, dique omnes noctis adeste,
> quorum ope, cum volui, ripis mirantibus amnes
> in fontes rediere suos, concussaque sisto,
> stantia concutio cantu freta, nubila pello
> nubilaque induco, ventos abigoque vocoque,
> vipereas rumpo verbis et carmine fauces,
> vivaque saxa sua convulsaque robora terra
> et silvas moveo iubeoque tremescere montis
> et mugire solum manesque exire sepulcris!
> te quoque, Luna, traho, quamvis Temesaea labores
> aera tuos minuant; currus quoque carmine nostro
> pallet avi, pallet nostris Aurora venenis!

In Prospero's 'I have bedimm'd The noontide sun' (5, 1, 41–2), Shakespeare seems to have taken Golding's version 'Our sorcery dims the morning fair, and darks the sun at noon' (for 'currus quoque carmine nostro | pallet'), but 'by whose aid' (line 40) is a direct translation of 'quorum ope' and not a paraphrase of 'Through help of whom'.

D. Some of Shakespeare's original versions:

The dream-vision of Clarence in *Richard III, 1, 4, 24–32*

> . . . Methought I saw a thousand fearful wrecks;
> Ten thousand men that fishes gnaw'd upon;
> Wedges of gold, great anchors, heaps of pearl,
> Inestimable stones, unvalu'd jewels,
> All scatter'd in the bottom of the sea.
> Some lay in dead men's skulls, and in the holes
> Where eyes did once inhabit, there were crept—
> As 'twere in scorn of eyes—reflecting gems,
> That woo'd the slimy bottom of the deep,
> And mock'd the dead bones that lay scatter'd by.

A description of the perfect woman, *As You Like It*, *3*, *2*, 138–52:

> Therefore Heaven Nature charg'd
>   That one body should be fill'd
> With all graces wide enlarg'd:
>   Nature presently distill'd
> Helen's cheek but not her heart,
>   Cleopatra's majesty,
> Atalanta's better part,
>   Sad Lucretia's modesty.
> Thus Rosalind of many parts
>   By heavenly synod was devis'd,
> Of many faces, eyes, and hearts,
>   To have the touches dearest priz'd.
> Heaven would that she these gifts should have,
>   And I to live and die her slave.

The impatience of the bride, *Romeo and Juliet*, *3*, *2*, 1–4:

> Gallop apace, you fiery-footed steeds,
> Towards Phoebus' lodging; such a waggoner
> As Phaeton would whip you to the west,
> And bring in cloudy night immediately.

Enchantment and Ariel

A 'scientific' explanation and a 'romantic' appreciation

From Dr Samuel Johnson: editor, critic, poet, and scholar

That the Character and Conduct of Prospero may be understood, something must be known of the System of Enchantment, which supplied all the Marvellous found in the Romances of the Middle Ages. This system seems to have been founded on the Opinion that the fallen Spirits, having different degrees of guilt, had different Habitations allotted them on their Expulsion, some being confined in Hell, some . . . dispersed in Air, some on Earth, some in Water, others in Caves, Dens or Minerals under the Earth. Of these some were more malignant and mischievous than others. The earthy Spirits seem to have been thought the most depraved, and the aerial the least vitiated. Thus Prospero observes of Ariel,

> . . . thou wast a spirit too delicate
> To act her earthy and abhorred commands.

Over these Spirits a Power might be obtained by certain Rites performed or Charms learned. This Power was called the *Black Art* or *Knowledge of Enchantment*. The Enchanter being, as King James observes in his *Demonology*, one who commands the Devil, whereas the Witch serves him.

Those who thought best of this Art, the Existence of which was, I am afraid, believed very seriously, held that certain Sounds and Characters had a physical Power over Spirits, and compelled their Agency; others who condemned the Practice, which in reality was surely never practised, were of Opinion, with more Reason, that the Power of Charms arose only from compact, and was no more than the Spirits voluntary allowed them for the Seduction of Man. The Art was held by all, though not equally criminal yet unlawful . . . Thus Prospero repents of his Art in the last Scene. The Spirits were always considered as in some Measure enslaved to the Enchanter, at least for a Time, and as serving with

Unwillingness, therefore Ariel so often begs for Liberty; and Caliban observes that the Spirits serve Prospero with no good Will, but hate him rootedly.

—Of these Trifles enough.

'Notes on the Plays' from Dr Johnson's edition of
Shakespeare's *Works* (1765)

From Samuel Taylor Coleridge: poet, philosopher, and critic

. . . If a doubt could ever be entertained whether Shakespeare was a great poet, acting upon laws arising out of his own nature . . . that doubt must be removed by the character of Ariel. The very first words uttered by this being introduce the spirit, not as an angel, above man; not a gnome, or a fiend, below man; but whilst the poet gives him the faculties and the advantages of reason, he divests him of all mortal character, not positively, it is true, but negatively. In air he lives, from air he derives his being, in air he acts; and all his colours and properties seem to have been obtained from the rainbow and the skies. There is nothing about Ariel that cannot be conceived to exist either at sun-rise or at sun-set: hence all that belongs to Ariel belongs to the delight the mind is capable of receiving from the most lovely external appearances. His answers to Prospero are directly to the question, and nothing beyond; or where he expatiates, which is not unfrequently, it is to himself and upon his own delights, or upon the unnatural situation in which he is placed, though under a kindly power and to good ends.

Shakespeare has properly made Ariel's first speech characteristic of him. After he has described the manner in which he had raised the storm and produced its harmless consequences, we find that Ariel is discontented—that he has been freed, it is true, from a cruel confinement, but still that he is bound to obey Prospero and to execute any commands imposed upon him. We feel that such a state of bondage is almost unnatural to him, yet we see that it is delightful for him to be so employed.—It is as if we were to command one of the winds in a different direction to that which nature dictates, or one of the waves, now rising and now sinking, to recede before it breaks upon the shore: such is the feeling we experience, when we learn that a being like Ariel is commanded to fulfil any mortal behest.

When, however, Shakespeare contrasts the treatment of Ariel by Prospero with that of Sycorax, we are sensible that the liberated spirit ought to be grateful, and Ariel does feel and acknowledge the obligation; he immediately assumes the airy being, with a mind so elastically correspondent, that when once a feeling has passed from it, not a trace is left behind.

Is there anything in nature from which Shakespeare caught the idea of this delicate and delightful being, with such child-like simplicity, yet with such preternatural powers? He is neither born of heaven, nor of earth but, as it were, between both, like a May-blossom kept suspended in air by the fanning breeze, which prevents it from falling to the ground, and only finally, and by compulsion, touching earth. This reluctance of the Sylph to be under the command even of Prospero is kept up through the whole play, and in the exercise of his admirable judgement Shakespeare has availed himself of it, in order to give Ariel an interest in the event, looking forward to that moment when he was to gain his last and only reward—simple and eternal liberty.

'An Analysis of Act I of *The Tempest*' (1811), reprinted in *'The Tempest': a Casebook*, ed. D.J. Palmer (1968)

U. A. Fanthorpe: The Heir

It was very quiet on the island after
They all went back to Milan. Sounds
And sweet airs dwindled and petered out
As the fleet dissolved on Ariel's calm sea.

Caliban missed the music, being
A susceptible monster. The whole island
Was his now, sun, moon and yellow sands,
Filberts and freshets, but somehow

Vacant, and not worth having. Twangling
Instruments and spiteful hedgehogs
In retrospect mingled. He didn't know
Exactly what he was missing,

But he missed it. Prospero, he thought,
Had shipped harmony with the baggage
Back to Milan. Poor mooncalf, he didn't realize
They had all gone back to invest

In Olivetti and Neapolitan
Ice cream, abandoning magic
And music together. Only Ariel
Went on playing for love, and he never

Touched down on the island again.
His memories were quite distinct, and all
Of tyranny. So the island was soundless, airless,
Dumb to name Caliban king.[1]

[1] 'The Heir' by U. A. Fanthorpe, from *The Crystal Zoo* published by Oxford University Press, 1985, reprinted by permission of the author.

Music in *The Tempest*

The Tempest is the most musical of all Shakespeare's plays, demanding at least four singers for the roles of Ariel, Caliban, Stephano, and Trinculo (two of whom might 'double' for the goddesses in *Act 4*), dancers for the betrothal masque, and instrumentalists to accompany the songs and to play 'mood' music at crucial moments throughout the performance. The original settings still survive for two of Ariel's songs—'Full fathom five thy father lies' (*1*, 2, 397–405) and 'Where the bee sucks' (*5*, 1, 88–94)—and are the compositions of Robert Johnson, chief lutenist at the court of James I. Johnson also wrote a piece of dance music entitled 'The Tempest' which some critics assume to have been intended for Shakespeare's play—although dance music usually carries the name of the dance (or the dancer) and there is no specifically 'tempest-dance' here. Associated with the King's Men through his position at court, Johnson is known to have composed instrumental music for Ben Jonson's masque *Oberon* (1611) as well as vocal music for plays by Jonson and other of Shakespeare's contemporary dramatists but his speciality, according to his editor Ian Spink, was music for 'supernatural or otherwise bizarre dances'.

Full fathom five

S. & B. 5513

WHERE THE BEE SUCKS

Where the bee sucks there suck I,_____ In a cow-slip's

bell I lie, There I couch when owls do cry, On the

bat's back I do fly Af - ter sum - mer mer - ri - ly.

     S. & B. 5513

Classwork and Examinations

The plays of Shakespeare are studied all over the world, and this classroom edition is being used in many different countries. Teaching methods vary from school to school and there are many different ways of examining a student's work. Some teachers and examiners expect detailed knowledge of Shakespeare's text; others ask for imaginative involvement with his characters and their situations; and there are some teachers who want their students, by means of 'workshop' activities, to share in the theatrical experience of directing and performing a play. Most people use a variety of methods. This section of the book offers a few suggestions for approaches to *The Tempest* which could be used in schools and colleges to help with students' understanding and *enjoyment* of the play.

> A Discussion
> B Character Study
> C Activities
> D Context Questions
> E Comprehension Questions
> F Essays
> G Projects

A   Discussion

Talking about the play—about the issues it raises and the characters who are involved—is one of the most rewarding and pleasurable ways of studying Shakespeare. It makes sense to discuss each scene as it is read, sharing impressions—and perhaps correcting misapprehensions. It can be useful to compare aspects of this play with other fictions—plays, novels, films—or with modern life. A large class can divide into small groups, each with a leader, who can discuss different aspects of a single topic and then report back to the main assembly.

Suggestions

A1   Providence—Fate, Fortune, Destiny . . . Do you believe in *any* of these, or is it all random chance—and coincidence? Do you ever read your horoscope? Seriously?

A2 Monarchy, its privileges and responsibilities, are key issues in *The Tempest*. What are *your* views on the subject?

A3 ' . . . if a virgin, And your affections not gone forth, I'll make you The Queen of Naples' (*1*, 2, 448–50). How can a twentieth-century audience (or reader) be expected to respond to the play's obsession with Miranda's virginity?

A4 'This Is the third man that e'er I saw, the first That e'er I sigh'd for' (*1*, 2, 445–7). Do you believe in love at first sight?

A5 'All things in common nature should produce Without sweat or endeavour . . . ' What is your concept of the ideal commonwealth? How far do you agree with the ideas put forward by Gonzalo in *Act 2*, Scene 1, lines 156–65?

A6 'Sword, pike, knife, gun, or need of any engine Would I not have' (2, 1, 158–59). Would you be in favour of a total ban on all weapons?

A7 Prospero's educational theories seem to have been wasted on Caliban:

> A devil, a born devil, on whose nature
> Nurture can never stick; on whom my pains,
> Humanely taken, all, all lost, quite lost   (*4*, 1, 188–90)

Nature or nurture, birth or education—which do you think is the more important in life? Can we change our personalities and behaviour, or is everything predetermined by our genetic make-up?

A8 Caliban denounces Prospero as 'a tyrant . . . that by his cunning hath cheated me of the island'. Many indigenous peoples (Indian, Maori, Aboriginal) could say the same of the European settlers in their lands. Discuss the rights and wrongs of colonization.

B   Character Study

Shakespeare is famous for his creation of characters who seem like real people. We can judge their actions and we can try to comprehend their thoughts and feelings—just as we criticize and try to understand the people we know. As the play progresses, we learn to like or dislike, love or hate, them—just as though they lived in *our* world.

Characters can be studied *from the outside*, by observing what they do and listening sensitively to what they say. This is the scholar's method: the scholar—or any reader—has access to the entire play, and can see the function of every character within the whole scheme of that play.

Another approach works *from the inside*, taking a single character and looking at the action and the other characters from his/her point of view. This is the way an actor prepares for performance, creating a personality who can have only a partial notion of what is going on, and it asks for a student's inventive imagination and creative writing.

The two methods—both useful in different ways—are really complementary to each other, and for both of them it can be very helpful to re-frame the character's speeches *in your own words*, using the vocabulary and idiom of everyday parlance.

Suggestions

a) from 'outside' the character

B1 The emergency of the storm brings out the real self in every one of the characters. Show how far this is true of

a) Alonso
b) Gonzalo
c) Sebastian and Antonio.

B2 Listen very critically to Prospero's account of his own and his brother's conduct in Milan, then describe the changes in your reactions to one or both of the characters.

B3 Is Miranda an intriguingly complex character—or just inconsistently drawn?

B4 Can you find it in your heart to sympathize with Caliban?

B5 How would you describe the characters and functions of Stephano and Trinculo?

B6 The 'brave new world' (5, 1, 183) must begin with Ferdinand: show how, in the space of three hours, he must demonstrate his fitness to be King of Naples, husband of Miranda, and son-in-law to Prospero.

B7 Compare and contrast the characters of Antonio and Sebastian.

B8 Remembering that the spirit has neither shape nor form, attempt to give a description of Ariel to someone who has not seen or read the play.

b) from 'inside' the character

B9 In the character of the Boatswain, write an account of the storm and its aftermath for the benefit of one of the following:

    a) the ship's owners
    b) the local newspaper
    c) your wife

B10 'The government I cast upon my brother, And to my state grew stranger' (1, 2, 75–6). How would Antonio have described this state of affairs in a letter to the King of Naples (who was 'an enemy . . . inveterate' to Prospero)?

B11 Ferdinand is obviously highly skilled in the matters of courtship: write the love-letters or the poems that he would have sent to Miranda if there had been time for a longer engagement.

B12 'My island in the sun'. Write a song of praise in any form (ballad, blues, rap) to be sung by Caliban, who is obviously proud of his island and his knowledge of its resources. Alternatively, assuming that Prospero has managed to teach him to write, devise the holiday brochure that he might produce to attract tourists after Prospero has sailed back to Naples.

B13 'My life with father'—compose extracts from the memoirs of Queen Miranda of Naples *or* write the teenager's diary when her emotions are divided between love for the new boyfriend and fear of her father.

B14 'Were I in England now, as once I was, and had but this fish painted, not a holiday-fool there but would give a piece of silver' (2, 2, 27–9). Write the fairground 'spiel' for Stephano and Trinculo as they prepare to display the 'fish' they have brought back from their expedition.

B15 'The truth must be told': Alonso confesses the details of his conspiracy against Prospero.

B16 Antonio speaks few words—but what are his thoughts? Write a stream-of-consciousness monologue for him as Prospero reveals himself as Duke of Milan and explains what has been happening.

B17 Gonzalo welcomes the strange turn of events:

Was Milan thrust from Milan that his issue
Should become kings of Naples?

Write *either* his sermon on the workings of divine Providence, *or* the private diary in which he has been jotting down notes ever since he arrived on the island.

B18 As the ship sails towards Naples, all the characters have plenty of time to ponder over their sojourn on the island and to put their thoughts down on paper, in different ways and for different sorts of readers (diary, letter, newspaper article, poem). Write some of these.

B19 'The Heir', a poem by U. A. Fanthorpe (see p. 98), suggests that Caliban was left on the island when everyone else sailed back to Naples—but suppose he had gone with them! Write your own story about Caliban in the new world of Naples and Milan.

B20 Nowhere in the play is there opportunity for Prospero to voice his most private emotions in the most personal of dramatic forms, the soliloquy. Give him such an opportunity.

C   Activities

These can involve two or more students, preferably working *away from* the desk or study-table. They can help students to develop a sense of drama and the dramatic aspects of Shakespeare's play—which was written to be *performed*, not read!

Suggestions

C1   Act the play—or at least part of it! Experiment with different methods of staging the first scene—minimalist (bare stage, no props), conventional (scenery and costume), hi-tech. (all light and sound resources) etc. Transpose the action to the twentieth century, setting the scene in an airliner about to crash.

C2   Devise an action in mime to accompany Prospero's long speech in *Act 1*, Scene 2 for the better understanding of the deaf or audiences unfamiliar with the English language.

C3   Milan–Naples alliance! Antonio for duke! Government reshuffle! Nowadays such a political manoeuvre would be given full media coverage, with considerable debate about the principles and personalities involved and much speculation about the likely outcome. Transpose the events that Prospero describes to Miranda into the twentieth century and supply this cover, using the techniques of television, radio, and newspaper—both *The Times* and the *Sun*. Feature Antonio's justification of his actions, and interview the citizens to get their opinions on the situation.

C4 Remembering their comments on Prospero's island *(Act 2,* Scene 1), enact the scene that might develop if Alonso and Gonzalo, Sebastian and Antonio, were all to arrive at the same holiday resort.

C5 Perform the courtship scene between Ferdinand and Miranda using your own words and phraseology. What task could a twentieth-century father set to 'test' a prospective son-in-law?

C6 Celebrate the engagement of a modern couple whose alliance will also have political and/or financial implications for their parents' families/countries/businesses.

C7 Prospero seems to be suggesting a kind of 'soap-opera' as the ideal medium for his story—''tis a chronicle of day by day, Not a relation for a breakfast' (5, 1, 163–4). Design some brief episodes, giving each one the conventional 'cliff-hanger' closure.

C8   the isle is full of noises,
   Sounds, and sweet airs, that give delight and hurt not.

A popular BBC radio programme is *Desert Island Discs* where an imaginary 'castaway' is questioned about him/herself and chooses eight discs that he/she would like to take to a desert island. Interview any one of the play's characters on this programme. A single 'luxury' item is also allowed, and the 'castaway' may take one book of his/her own choice (the Bible and the works of Shakespeare are already on the island).

D   Context Questions

In written examinations, these questions present you with short passages from the play and ask you to explain them. They are intended to test your knowledge of the play and your understanding of its words. Usually you have to make a choice of passages: there may be five on the paper, and you are asked to choose three. Be very sure that you know exactly how many passages you must choose. Study the ones offered to you, and select those you feel most certain of. Make your answers accurate and concise—don't waste time writing more than the examiner is asking for.

D1 A devil, a born devil, on whose nature
Nurture can never stick; on whom my pains,
Humanely taken, all, all lost, quite lost;
And as with age his body uglier grows,
So his mind cankers. I will plague them all,
Even to roaring.

(i) Who is the 'devil' referred to in these lines and who was his mother?
(ii) Who is the speaker, and what 'pains' has he taken?
(iii) Who are the persons referred to as 'them', and what are they planning to do?

D2 Be not afeard, the isle is full of noises,
Sounds, and sweet airs, that give delight and hurt not.
Sometimes a thousand twangling instruments
Will hum about mine ears.

(i) Who is speaking and who is making the music?
(ii) Who is afraid of the sound of music? Why?
(iii) What do the characters plan to do? Are they successful?

D3 If he were that which now he's like—that's dead—
Whom I with this obedient steel, three inches of it,
Can lay to bed for ever; whiles you, doing thus,
To the perpetual wink for aye might put
This ancient morsel, this Sir Prudence.

(i) Who is 'he' and why does he appear to be dead?
(ii) Who is the speaker of these lines, and to whom does he speak?
(iii) Who is the 'ancient morsel'?
(iv) What is being planned—and what actually happens?

D4 Thou and thy meaner fellows your last service
Did worthily perform, and I must use you
In such another trick. Go, bring the rabble
O'er whom I give thee pow'r here to this place.

(i) Who is addressed here, and what is the 'rabble'?
(ii) What has been performed? For whose benefit?
(iii) Who is the speaker and what is the next 'trick' that he is planning?

D5   Old lord, I cannot blame thee,
Who am myself attach'd with weariness
To th' dulling of my spirits. Sit down and rest.

Even here I will put off my hope, and keep it
No longer for my flatterer.

   (i) Who is the 'Old lord' and why is he tired?
  (ii) What is the name and title of the speaker?
 (iii) What was he hoping for and was he right to despair?

E   Comprehension Questions

These also present passages from the play and ask questions about
them; again you often have a choice of passages. But the extracts
are much longer than those presented as context questions. A
detailed knowledge of the language of the play is required here, and
you must be able to express unusual or archaic phrases in your own
words; you may also be expected to comment critically on the
dramatic techniques of the passage and the poetic effectiveness of
Shakespeare's language.

E1   Prospero

                        Hear a little further,
And then I'll bring thee to the present business
Which now's upon 's; without the which this story
Were most impertinent.

    Miranda

                      Wherefore did they not
That hour destroy us?

    Prospero

                 Well demanded, wench: 5
My tale provokes that question. Dear, they durst not,
So dear the love my people bore me, nor set
A mark so bloody on the business; but
With colours fairer painted their foul ends.
In few, they hurried us aboard a barque,   10
Bore us some leagues to sea, where they prepar'd
A rotten carcass of a butt, not rigg'd,
Nor tackle, sail, nor mast—the very rats
Instinctively have quit it. There they hoist us
To cry to th' sea that roar'd to us, to sigh   15
To th' winds, whose pity, sighing back again,
Did us but loving wrong.

    Miranda

                  Alack, what trouble
Was I then to you!

Prospero
                    O, a cherubin
Thou wast that did preserve me. Thou didst smile,
Infused with a fortitude from heaven,   20
When I have deck'd the sea with drops full salt,
Under my burden groan'd, which rais'd in me
An undergoing stomach to bear up
Against what should ensue.
            Miranda
                              How came we ashore?
            Prospero
By providence divine.   25

(i)   What is meant by '*impertinent*' (line 4); '*colours*' (line 9);
      '*rigg'd*' (line 12); '*deck'd*' (line 21); '*full salt*' (line 21)?
(ii) Express in your own words the full meaning of lines 22–4,
      'Under . . . ensue'.
(iii) Comment on Shakespeare's narrative skills in this passage.
(iv) What do these lines show you about the characters
      speaking?

E2   **Prospero**

                    Soft, sir, one word more.
[*Aside*] They are both in either's powers; but this swift
    business
I must uneasy make lest too light winning
Make the prize light.—One word more: I charge thee
That thou attend me. Thou dost here usurp   5
The name thou ow'st not, and hast put thyself
Upon this island as a spy, to win it
From me, the lord on't.
            Ferdinand
                              No, as I am a man!
            Miranda
There's nothing ill can dwell in such a temple.
If the ill spirits have so fair a house,   10
Good things will strive to dwell with't.
            Prospero
                                        Follow me.—
Speak not you for him: he's a traitor.—Come,
I'll manacle thy neck and feet together.
Sea-water shalt thou drink; thy food shall be

The fresh-brook mussels, withered roots, and husks 15
Wherein the acorn cradled. Follow.

Ferdinand
                                        No;
I will resist such entertainment till
Mine enemy has more power.

He draws, and is charmed from moving

Miranda
                                O dear father,
Make not too rash a trial of him, for
He's gentle, and not fearful.

Prospero
                                What, I say— 20
My foot my tutor? Put thy sword up, traitor,
Who mak'st a show but dar'st not strike, thy conscience
Is so possess'd with guilt. Come from thy ward,
For I can here disarm thee with this stick
And make thy weapon drop.

Miranda
                                Beseech you, father— 25

Prospero
Hence! Hang not on my garments.

Miranda
                                Sir, have pity;
I'll be his surety.

Prospero
                Silence! One word more
Shall make me chide thee, if not hate thee. What,
An advocate for an impostor? Hush!
Thou think'st there is no more such shapes as he, 30
Having seen but him and Caliban. Foolish wench,
To th' most of men this is a Caliban,
And they to him are angels.

Miranda
                                My affections
Are then most humble. I have no ambition
To see a goodlier man.

(i) What is meant by '*attend*' (line 5); '*entertainment*' (line 17);
    '*ward*' (line 23); '*surety*' (line 27).

(ii) In your own words, express the meaning of 'this swift business . . . light' (lines 2–4); 'nothing ill . . . temple' (line 9); 'My foot my tutor' (line 21).

(iii) Comment on the dramatic qualities of Shakespeare's verse in this episode.

(iv) What does this episode show you of the characters and their relationships with each other?

F   Essays

These will usually give you a specific topic to discuss, or perhaps a question that must be answered, in writing, *with a reasoned argument*. They *never* want you to tell the story of the play—so don't! Your examiner—or teacher—has read the play, and does not need to be reminded of it. Relevant quotations will always help you to make your points more strongly.

F1 'Shakespeare compresses the material for a whole tragedy into a single scene of his comedy.' Show how this is done.

F2 'The government I cast upon my brother, And to my state grew stranger' (*1, 2, 75–6*). It might be argued that Prospero was criminally negligent and well deserved to lose his dukedom. Would you agree?

F3 'The lust for power is common to all men: even Gonzalo would be king of his commonwealth.' Compare any two or three characters in *The Tempest* in their attitudes to power.

F4 'Freedom, high-day! High-day, freedom.' Ariel and Caliban both long for freedom—but their ideas are very different. Contrast their attitudes to freedom and servitude.

F5 The most musical of Shakespeare's plays—but the music is never mere decoration. Discuss some of the functions of music in *The Tempest*.

F6 A therapeutic experience! According to Gonzalo, the experience on the island had proved to be one of self-discovery, in the course of which all the characters had found their true selves, 'When no man was his own' (5, 1, 213). How far would you agree with this?

G   Projects

In some schools, students are required to do more 'free-ranging' work, which takes them outside the text—but which should always be relevant to the play. Such Projects may demand skills other than reading and writing: design and artwork, for instance, may be involved. Sometimes a 'portfolio' of work is assembled over a considerable period of time; and this can be offered to the examiner for assessment.

The availability of resources will, obviously, do much to determine the nature of the Projects; but this is something that only the local teachers will understand. However, there is always help to be found in libraries, museums, and art galleries.

Suggested Subjects

G1   Elizabethan magic.

G2   The masque.

G3   The New World: colonization in the early seventeenth century.

G4   Who played Prospero? Great actors of the past.

G5   Utopia—or the ideal commonwealth.

G6   Images of Ariel.

G7   Images of Caliban.

Background

England c. *1611*

When Shakespeare was writing *The Tempest*, many people still believed that the sun went round the earth. They were taught that this was a divinely ordered scheme of things, and that—in England—God had instituted a Church and ordained a Monarchy for the right government of the land and the populace.

'The past is a foreign country; they do things differently there.'

L. P. Hartley

Government

For most of Shakespeare's life, the reigning monarch of England was Queen Elizabeth I: when she died, she was succeeded by King James I. He was also king of Scotland (James VI), and the two kingdoms were united in 1603 by his accession to the English throne. With his counsellors and ministers, James governed the nation (population less than six million) from London, although fewer than half a million people inhabited the capital city. In the rest of the country, law and order were maintained by the land-owners and enforced by their deputies. The average man had no vote, and his wife had no rights at all.

Religion

At this time, England was a Christian country. All children were baptized, soon after they were born, into the Church of England; they were taught the essentials of the Christian faith, and instructed in their duty to God and to humankind. Marriages were performed, and funerals conducted, only by the licensed clergy and in accordance with the Church's rites and ceremonies. Attendance at divine service was compulsory; absences (without good—medical—reason) could be punished by fines. By such means, the authorities were able to keep some check on the populace—recording births, marriages, and deaths; being alert to any religious nonconformity, which could be politically dangerous; and ensuring a minimum of orthodox instruction through the official 'Homilies' which were regularly preached from the pulpits of all parish churches throughout the realm.

Following Henry VIII's break away from the Church of Rome, all people in England were able to hear the church services *in their own language*. The Book of Common Prayer was used in every church, and an English translation of the Bible was read aloud in public. The Christian religion had never been so well taught before!

Education

School education reinforced the Church's teaching. From the age of four, boys might attend the 'petty school' (French '*petite école*') to learn the rudiments of reading and writing along with a few prayers; some schools also included work with numbers. At the age of seven, the boy was ready for the grammar school (if his father was willing and able to pay the fees).

Here, a thorough grounding in Latin grammar was followed by translation work and the study of Roman authors, paying attention as much to style as to matter. The arts of fine writing were thus inculcated from early youth. A very few students proceeded to university; these were either clever scholarship boys, or else the sons of noblemen. Girls stayed at home, and acquired domestic and social skills—cooking, sewing, perhaps even music. The lucky ones might learn to read and write.

Language

At the start of the sixteenth century the English had a very poor opinion of their own language: there was little serious writing in English, and hardly any literature. Latin was the language of international scholarship, and Englishmen admired the eloquence of the Romans. They made many translations, and in this way they extended the resources of their own language, increasing its vocabulary and stretching its grammatical structures. French, Italian, and Spanish works were also translated and, for the first time, there were English versions of the Bible. By the end of the century, English was a language to be proud of: it was rich in synonyms, capable of infinite variety and subtlety, and ready for all kinds of word-play—especially the *puns*, for which Elizabethan English is renowned.

Drama

The great art-form of the Elizabethan and Jacobean age was its drama. The Elizabethans inherited a tradition of play-acting from the Middle Ages, and they reinforced this by reading and translating the Roman playwrights. At the beginning of the sixteenth century plays were performed by groups of actors, all-male companies (boys acted the female roles) who travelled from town to town, setting up their stages in open places (such as inn-yards) or, with the permission of the owner, in the hall of some noble house. The touring companies continued in the provinces into the seventeenth century; but in London, in 1576, a new building was erected for the performance of plays. This was the Theatre, the first purpose-built playhouse in England. Other playhouses followed, (including the Globe, where most of Shakespeare's plays were performed), and the English drama reached new heights of eloquence.

There were those who disapproved, of course. The theatres, which brought large crowds together, could encourage the spread of disease—and dangerous ideas. During the summer, when the plague was at its worst, the playhouses were closed. A constant censorship was imposed, more or less severe at different times. The Puritan faction tried to close down the theatres, but—partly because there was royal favour for the drama, and partly because the buildings were outside the city limits—they did not succeed until 1642.

Theatre

From contemporary comments and sketches—most particularly a drawing by a Dutch visitor, Johannes de Witt—it is possible to form some idea of the typical Elizabethan playhouse for which most of Shakespeare's plays were written. Hexagonal in shape, it had three roofed galleries encircling an open courtyard. The plain, high stage projected into the yard, where it was surrounded by the audience of standing 'groundlings'. At the back were two doors for the actors' entrances and exits; and above these doors was a balcony—useful for a musicians' gallery or for the acting of scenes '*above*'. Over the stage was a thatched roof, supported on two pillars, forming a canopy—which seems to have been painted with the sun, moon, and stars for the 'heavens'.

Underneath was space (concealed by curtaining) which could be used by characters ascending and descending through a trapdoor in the stage. Costumes and properties were kept backstage, in the 'tiring house'. The actors dressed lavishly, often wearing the secondhand clothes bestowed by rich patrons. Stage properties were important for defining a location, but the dramatist's own words were needed to explain the time of day, since all performances took place in the early afternoon.

Further Reading

Editions:

Excellent introductions to *The Tempest* are to be found in:

Kermode, Frank (ed.), *The Tempest* (Arden Shakespeare, London, 1954).
Righter, Anne (Barton) (ed.), *The Tempest* (New Penguin Shakespeare, Harmondsworth, 1968).

Critical Works:

Clark, Sandra, *The Tempest* (Penguin Critical Studies, Harmondsworth, 1986).
Edwards, Philip, 'Shakespeare's Romances: 1900–1957', *Shakespeare Survey 11* (1958), pp. 1–18.
Fry, Northrop, *A Natural Perspective: The Development of Shakespearean Comedy and Romance* (New York, 1955).
James, D. G., *The Dream of Prospero* (Oxford, 1967).
—— 'The Failure of the Ballad-Makers', in *Scepticism and Poetry: An Essay on the Poetic Imagination* (London, 1937), 205–41.
Knight, G. Wilson, *The Crown of Life: Essays in the Interpretation of Shakespeare's Final Plays* (London, 1947).
Pettet, E. C., *Shakespeare and the Romance Tradition* (London, 1949).
Ristine, F. H., *English Tragicomedy: Its Origin and History* (New York, 1910).
Sanders, Norman, 'An Overview of Critical Approaches to the Romances', in *Shakespeare's Romances Reconsidered*, ed. C. M. Kay and H. E. Jacobs (Lincoln, Nebr., 1978), 1–10.
Sisson, C. J., 'The Magic of Prospero', *Shakespeare Survey 11* (1958), 70–7.
Stoll, E. E., 'The Tempest', *Publications of the Modern Language Association of America* 47 (1932), 699–726.
Tillyard, E. M. W., *Shakespeare's Last Plays* (London, 1938).
Traversi, Derek A., *Shakespeare: The Last Phase* (London, 1954).

Wells, Stanley, 'Shakespeare and Romance', in *The Later Shakespeare*, ed. John Russell Brown and Bernard Harris (Stratford-Upon-Avon Studies, 8; London, 1966), 49–79.

Palmer, D. J., *Shakespeare: 'The Tempest', a Casebook* (London, 1968).

Sources:

The most complete study of the sources of *The Tempest* is to be found in:

Bullough, Geoffrey (ed.), *Narrative and Dramatic Sources of Shakespeare*, 8 vols (London, 1957–75), vol. 8.

Additional background reading:

Blake, N. F., *Shakespeare's Language: an Introduction*, (London, 1983).

Muir, K., and Schoenbaum, S., *A New Companion to Shakespeare Studies* (Cambridge, 1971).

Schoenbaum, S., *William Shakespeare: A Documentary Life* (Oxford, 1975).

Thomson, Peter, *Shakespeare's Theatre* (London, 1983).

William Shakespeare, 1564–1616

Elizabeth I was Queen of England when Shakespeare was born in 1564. He was the son of a tradesman who made and sold gloves in the small town of Stratford-upon-Avon, and he was educated at the grammar school in that town. Shakespeare did not go to university when he left school, but worked, perhaps in his father's business. When he was eighteen he married Anne Hathaway, who became the mother of his daughter, Susanna, in 1583, and of twins in 1585.

There is nothing exciting, or even unusual, in this story; and from 1585 until 1592 there are no documents that can tell us anything at all about Shakespeare. But we have learned that in 1592 he was known in London, and that he had become both an actor and a playwright.

We do not know when Shakespeare wrote his first play, and indeed we are not sure of the order in which he wrote his works. If you look on page 124 at the list of his writings and their approximate dates, you will see how he started by writing plays on subjects taken from the history of England. No doubt this was partly because he was always an intensely patriotic man—but he was also a very shrewd business-man. He could see that the theatre audiences enjoyed being shown their own history, and it was certain that he would make a profit from this kind of drama.

The plays in the next group are mainly comedies, with romantic love-stories of young people who fall in love with one another, and at the end of the play marry and live happily ever after.

At the end of the sixteenth century the happiness disappears, and Shakespeare's plays become melancholy, bitter, and tragic. This change may have been caused by some sadness in the writer's life (one of his twins died in 1596). Shakespeare, however, was not the only writer whose works at this time were very serious. The whole of England was facing a crisis. Queen Elizabeth I was growing old. She was greatly loved, and the people were sad to think she must soon die; they were also afraid, for the queen had never married, and so there was no child to succeed her.

When James I came to the throne in 1603, Shakespeare continued to write serious drama—the great tragedies and the plays based on Roman history (such as *Julius Caesar*) for which he is most famous. Finally, before he retired from the theatre, he wrote another set of comedies. These all have the same theme: they tell of happiness which is lost, and then found again.

Shakespeare returned from London to Stratford, his home town. He was rich and successful, and he owned one of the biggest houses in the town. He died in 1616.

Shakespeare also wrote two long poems, and a collection of sonnets. The sonnets describe two love-affairs, but we do not know who the lovers were. Although there are many public documents concerned with his career as a writer and a business-man, Shakespeare has hidden his personal life from us. A nineteenth-century poet, Matthew Arnold, addressed Shakespeare in a poem, and wrote, 'We ask and ask—Thou smilest, and art still'.

There is not even a trustworthy portrait of the world's greatest dramatist.

Approximate order of composition of Shakespeare's works

Period	Comedies	History plays	Tragedies	Poems
I	Comedy of Errors	Henry VI, part 1	Titus Andronicus	
	Taming of the Shrew	Henry VI, part 2		
	Two Gentlemen of Verona	Henry VI, part 3		
		Richard III		
		King John		
1594	Love's Labour's Lost			Venus and Adonis
				Rape of Lucrece
II	Midsummer Night's Dream	Richard II	Romeo and Juliet	Sonnets
	Merchant of Venice	Henry IV, part 1		
	Merry Wives of Windsor	Henry IV, part 2		
	Much Ado About Nothing			
1599	As You Like It	Henry V		
III	Twelfth Night		Julius Caesar	
	Troilus and Cressida		Hamlet	
	Measure for Measure		Othello	
1608	All's Well That Ends Well		Timon of Athens	
			King Lear	
			Macbeth	
			Antony and Cleopatra	
			Coriolanus	
IV	Pericles			
	Cymbeline			
	The Winter's Tale	Henry VIII		
1613	The Tempest			